RUNNING SCARED

Running Scared

Robert Leon Davis

For 22 years a fugitive - the
corrupt cop busted by God

MONARCH
BOOKS

Oxford, UK & Grand Rapids, Michigan, USA

First published in the UK in 2010 by Monarch Books
(a publishing imprint of Lion Hudson plc)
Wilkinson House, Jordan Hill Road, Oxford OX2 8DR, England
Tel: +44 (0)1865 302750 Fax: +44 (0)1865 302757
Email: monarch@lionhudson.com
www.lionhudson.com

ISBN 978 1 85424 993 7

Distributed by:
UK: Marston Book Services, PO Box 269, Abingdon, Oxon OX14 4YN
USA: Kregel Publications, PO Box 2607, Grand Rapids, Michigan 49501

Published in association with the literary agency of Credo Communications LLC, Grand Rapids, Michigan.

British Library Cataloguing Data

A catalogue record for this book is available from the British Library.

Printed and bound in Great Britain by the MPG Books Group

In memory of my Grandma,
Tessie Jones

Contents

Foreword

In 2007 I celebrated my fiftieth year as a priest, my Golden Jubilee. The majority of those years were spent at Holy Angels Church on the south side of Chicago, Illinois. The rectory of the church had a threshold at the front door that experienced thousands upon thousands of footsteps. I was the Pastor of Holy Angels and I opened that rectory door countless times to numerous folk from all walks of life.

The most unforgettable character ever to enter through that rectory doorway was Robert Davis, whom I call Bobby. His story is so outlandish that anyone hearing it would have no choice but to be highly skeptical. When I first met him, Bobby unraveled a tale that was simply unbelievable, incredible, astounding and beyond belief!

He stated he was a former police officer from New Orleans, Louisiana, who had become involved in a major crime. Fearing conviction, he fled to Canada and lived a homeless existence for some years in the Canadian woods. I am a consummate realist who found his story too hard to swallow. Having heard so many "stories" at that rectory door, I found Bobby Davis' spiel to be unbelievable, but highly intriguing. I mused, "How could anyone have the audacious effrontery to bring such a madcap account to me?"

Gradually, however, Bobby not only became an integral part of the life of Holy Angels, but he also entered into my heart. As time went by, my skepticism became challenged more and more. I found myself becoming not just simply a friend to Bobby, but also his confidant.

I urge readers of this amazing autobiography to lower their

guard. They will find, as I did, that Bobby Davis is telling the truth, the whole truth. His story is one of unvarnished honesty. Bobby has written a book that literally grips the soul. It is difficult to put this book down once it has been picked up.

My friendship with Bobby is certainly one of the highlights of my fifty years in the priesthood. I thank Almighty God for that momentous day when Bobby crossed the threshold of Holy Angels Rectory. The years have taken their toll, but they will never dim the brightness of our friendship. Read this book. You will love this story of victory over incredible odds. *Running Scared* is the true story of a cop who came in!

Father George Clements
Chicago, Illinois

Acknowledgments

I would like to thank the following people:

My brothers and sisters for their ongoing love and support.

My mother for giving me birth through God.

My Uncle Andrew and Aunt Dee for moral support.

My Aunt Beulah and my cousin Ethel for that special gift.

My Aunt Delores for a special talk we had.

Also, my cousin Alana for sharing true friendship.

There are a few people to whom I wish to give special thanks. Thank you, Father Clements, for your guidance and godly wisdom. Thanks to Carol Foster and her assistant Candi, who were instrumental in transcribing the early phases of my manuscript. Thanks to several friends who reviewed the drafts and provided helpful comments about the content. Thank you, Agent Darryl Anderson, for treating me with dignity and respect. Thanks to the Honorable Judge Sharon Hunter for your faith in my true repentance. A special thanks to my sister, Thecla, for permitting me to reside in her home during my surrendering process, and to my brother Tony for standing with me in court. Thanks to Dr Roxanne Davidson for her assistance and professional input.

I would also like to acknowledge the following people who gave me their assistance to get this book off the ground:

Literary agent David Sanford for his original assessment of my manuscript and deciding that it had merit. Literary agent Rebekah Clark for her tireless efforts to find the perfect publisher for this project and seeing it through to completion. Literary agent Karen Neumair for her expert representation of my writing endeavors going forward.

A special thanks to Credo Communications and Timothy J. Beal for representation and support. A warm thanks to Robert Michaels for his contributions to this project.

Most importantly, I thank God for keeping me safe in the forests and woods and for putting up with my ignorance for many years.

Robert Leon Davis

Introduction

As will become apparent to you as you read these reflections, I traveled almost constantly for a twenty-two-year period of my life. Because of this, I cannot always recall specific dates, months or years. In those areas where I am specific, it is due to the fact that I later contacted individuals I know to confirm my recollections. The time I spent with Father George Clements in Chicago was not easily forgettable and impacted me greatly.

In this book I have not been able to include details of every city or state I visited. I traveled to many places and passed through some of the same cities a few times. But those places in which my life was greatly impacted have been included. However, most of the names of the people in this book are fictitious, in order to protect the identities of the real individuals concerned.

Upon my eventual surrender to the authorities in New Orleans, Louisiana, I was reunited with my family – my brothers and sisters – in 2002, and I met several nephews and nieces for the first time. I would like to make it clear that I love my family very much. Although years separated us, I know they forgave me for being absent from their lives for so long. I realize if you want forgiveness, you must be prepared to forgive.

It has taken me four years of concentration and diligence to complete this book, and I would like to make one thing clear to the reader: I take sole responsibility and blame for all the wrongs I have done in my life. In no way do I wish to imply to the reader that I was a victim. Words cannot express my deep sorrow for the people I've hurt on this journey. Therefore, I wish to humbly say to them, "I am sorry. Please forgive me." I am sorry in a godly way, with sincerity and regret.

I sincerely hope that at least one police officer reading this book learns from my mistakes and upholds his sworn duty to protect and serve the public. Do not violate your oath as I shamefully did. There is, I am convinced, a God – a higher authority who loves us all.

Robert Leon Davis

*My grandma told us many
stories based on some
moral principle to get us
to live decently and to
remember her mantra: "Do
the right thing!"*

Chapter 1

New Orleans, Louisiana – the Early Years

I was born the eldest of nine children in a poor family living in New Orleans, Louisiana. We were raised by my maternal grandmother's sister (Aunt Tessie) in a very religious family. We attended church regularly, every Sunday. "Grandma", as we affectionately called Aunt Tessie, was a good person in every sense of the word. She was a God-fearing, loving woman trying to raise nine kids on a $300 welfare check. Granted, this was the 1970s and prices were much cheaper than they are today, but that amount of money just wasn't enough for so many kids. Somehow, she managed. We children understood this struggle and assisted Grandma with any extra money we could get our hands on.

We lived in an area of New Orleans called Hollygrove. It was a ghetto. Hollygrove was a crime-infested, drug-ridden haven for crooks and up-and-coming crooks. It was so bad, in fact, that if you took a twelve-year-old boy into that slum, dropped him off and returned seven days later to retrieve him, he would have become a fully fledged criminal. In the early seventies I was a criminal too. Any angle to make a fast dollar. My buddies and I roamed the streets of Hollygrove day and night looking for an easy hit.

How all nine children came to be raised by Grandma is unclear to this day, but I do know my father left the family when I was young and I have no memory of him. Being the oldest, I assume my siblings don't remember him either. What I do know, from family discussions, is that he was an orphan from the state of Texas. After being adopted, he served in the United States Air Force. His mother, whose name was Lydia, was unknown to me also, so Grandma was the only person in my life, besides my siblings, whom I knew intimately.

As we grew up in Hollygrove my mother lived on the other side of town and later moved to Baton Rouge. On occasion she would visit us at Grandma's house and some of us stayed with her for very short periods of time. I hardly knew anything about her other than she was a very intelligent woman and had a vast knowledge about many subjects, which always impressed me.

My siblings and I never knew what happened between my father and mother to cause their separation. My mother always appeared uncomfortable discussing the subject, so we often asked Grandma why we didn't stay with our father or mother. Grandma simply told us not to worry about that – end of discussion. Furthermore, she explained we were *her* children and reassured us that she would raise all of us. We wondered what was going on. Other families we saw – most of them, anyway – enjoyed having both parents under one roof. So despite Grandma's reassurances, I continually wondered, "Why don't we live with our parents?"

My siblings and I were a strong and feisty group. After me, the oldest was my brother Tony, an aspiring United States Army career soldier. Tony was exceptionally disciplined even as a child and was by far the quietest in the family. After Tony came my brother Kenth, who was similar in appearance to Jimmy Hendrix with long, black braided hair. He had a carefree, eccentric personality. Following Kenth was my brother Kwame. Kwame was a spontaneous character. Once, after watching the 1970s TV show *Kojak* starring Telly Savalas, he decided the next day to shave his head and walked around sporting a lollipop in his mouth! He could see a film about anything at all and want to be "that person". Next, my brother Keith was a ladies' man. All the girls floated towards him, not necessarily because of his looks (which he possessed), but because of his gift of the gab. The last of the boys was the "baby boy", Jack. He was a blend of us all and had an unpredictable nature – he might flip when you thought he would flop, or dive when you thought he would duck!

After the boys, my mother had three girls in succession. Valerie, the oldest girl, was the fighter. She wasn't scared of anyone or anything. Then there was my sister Vivian, who was sort of quiet and known as the practical one – logical, methodical, not careless or reckless. Finally, there was my sister with the unusual name – Thecla. She was the outright baby of the family. Thec (for short) was the girl that hung with the boys. She could play sports or complete a task just as skillfully as any boy. She had a very strong mind and was instrumental in helping me later in my life.

Grandma hustled constantly and did anything she could to feed, clothe and protect us. Physically she was an old, frail lady, but her belief in God carried her in life. Often, she would sit all nine kids around her in the living-room and tell us about all the things she went through as a young lady growing up in Denham Springs just outside Baton Rouge. During her twenties, Denham Springs was controlled and operated by the Ku Klux Klan and she told us stories of the rape and murder of her neighbors and friends by Klan members, as well as sharing family folklore and tales of survival against the odds.

Along with her accounts of real events, Grandma told us many parable-like stories to teach us moral principles. Once, after I had been late for school, I vividly remember her telling me a story – which was also related to the fact that I was known among my siblings for talking too much. Grandma said that bad things could happen to a person who didn't want to listen to instructions.

"Once, a flock of birds were up north with severe cold weather approaching," she told me. "All the birds got together and decided it was time to fly south. But this one bird decided to tell the flock to fly down and he would meet them later. The flock flew south while this one bird stayed behind to conduct other business. After his business was completed he started his flight south.

"By this time, about halfway through his journey, the air was bitterly cold and the bird's wings froze. Eventually he fell to the ground, unable to move with his frozen wings any more. After a few hours, a fox passed by and happened to squat down to release excrement on top of the unseen frozen bird. After a few seconds, the bird thawed and began tweeting and chirping happily. The fox looked behind, however, heard the chirping, noticed the bird and promptly devoured him."

In amazement, I questioned Grandma about the meaning of this tale. She looked at me sternly, bent towards me and said, "If someone tells you to do something urgently, do it! But if you delay and find yourself in trouble because of the delay, shut up!" I don't know whether Grandma made this story up specifically for me, but she had many similar tales to tell, based on some moral principle or other, designed to get us to live decently and to help us remember her mantra: *"Do the right thing!"*

Because times were so hard, on one occasion, when I was about fifteen, I convinced three of my younger brothers to assist me in robbing a small grocery store situated down the road from our home. Grandma was struggling to feed us, so I naively thought stealing from the store would help her. I informed my brothers of my plan, namely that we would go to bed as normal, around 10 p.m., and act as if we were sleeping, then meet on the back porch after Grandma was asleep.

We met at midnight, sneaked around the back of the store and managed to break into the storage area. We stole sodas, sweet potatoes, green beans, loaves of bread and packs of dried beans. Afterwards we hid these items in our home, even though we knew full well that Grandma was a very spiritual lady who would never approve of us stealing. Unfortunately for us, a neighbor called Mr. Hamilton had observed the burglary in progress and, unbeknown to us, called the New Orleans Police Department to report the crime.

In due course the police arrived with sirens wailing and emergency lights flashing. They came straight to Grandma's house and banged on the door. They woke up Grandma, who answered the door. The four of us were in bed, faking sleep. I overheard the police explaining to Grandma that an eyewitness had observed her grandchildren stealing. By this time, the owner of the store had also been woken by the police and summoned to the scene, and was standing in our living-room.

We were dragged out of bed and brought downstairs, and with Grandma's permission the police searched the house for the stolen goods and, of course, located them – everywhere! We had placed items in our closets, under our beds, behind the sofa and in various other places throughout the house.

Grandma was extremely hurt and angry that we would do such a thing. Of course, the worst thing you can do to an elderly lady at 1 a.m. is to wake her to discuss her grandsons' thievery!

Eventually all the neighbors were up and standing around outside, wondering what was going on, which was surely a terrible embarrassment to Grandma. The police officers discussed with the store owner the charges that would be brought against us, but miraculously he refused to take any legal action. Instead, he said all he wanted was for his stock to be returned and he would be happy with that resolution. Grandma then spoke privately with him. Following their discussion, they spoke to the police, who agreed not to arrest us. After the police left, Grandma informed us that we would return all the stolen items in the morning. We went back to bed, but hardly slept, terrified about what would happen the next day.

We conducted our crime on a Friday evening. This meant the next day was the weekend and all the neighborhood kids and adults were at home. At about 9 or 10 a.m. Grandma made the four of us gather together the stolen goods and carry them down the street, in broad daylight, back to the grocery store. The whole neighborhood came out to watch us do it, while Grandma directed us from the front porch. We were acutely embarrassed, while all our friends and neighbors stood by laughing and taunting us. As if that were not enough, when we returned, shame-faced, Grandma made each of us go inside, put on one of her dresses, and sit on the front porch in front of everyone for several hours! By the time she allowed us to return inside, suffice to say, none of us had the nerve to go outside for the remainder of the weekend.

As you can tell, Grandma did not play games. Under her stern influence, consisting of regular beatings and time out for misbehavior or being banned from playing outside, none of my guilty brothers stole again. Me, I was a little bit more evil or just stubborn. Instead of being reformed, I simply vowed I would never let her catch me stealing again.

My siblings and I tried to assist Grandma the legal way, by means such as delivering newspapers, babysitting and running errands, and this helped her some, but not enough. I came to believe that crooked money was faster and simpler to obtain. I could steal a car, strip it, sell the parts and make $500 for only five hours' work. In the mid 1970s $500 was plenty of money. If someone managed to do this several times a month, then it suddenly became a lot of money. In this way I supplemented Grandma's paltry $300-per-month income, easily doubling it. Though it was the wrong thing to do, I have no idea how our family would have survived if I hadn't.

In 1975 I was twenty years old. One day, I pondered what I would do with myself. I figured I couldn't pursue crime all my life, but I had no clue as to what else I could do. My only income was gained via car theft, my life was leading nowhere good, and I had to develop a plan to get out of the ghetto. I was the oldest kid in our family and I was supposed to be setting a good example for the others to follow. The problem was, I had no good example to follow myself. I kept thinking about how my father had left us when we were very young. "How could he abandon his wife and nine kids?" I wondered. It seemed a remarkably callous thing to do.

In those days, there was no such thing as mandatory child support either. Lucky him.

Chapter 2

New Orleans – on the Force

Next door to us were two brothers who, despite living in Hollygrove's epicenter of crime, somehow managed to escape being seduced into a life of crime by the local riff-raff. Their father was a police officer and their mother a county sheriff. Both boys had followed suit and become New Orleans police officers. They were good people and I couldn't fathom why they lived in Hollygrove; they were certainly out of place there. Suffice to say, their home was never burgled.

I became good friends with these brothers, Keith and Johnny, and used to hang out with them after they got off work. I don't know why, but they seemed to like me a lot and clearly cared about what might happen to me. Because of this, each evening I had to endure a lengthy lecture about the virtues of honesty. They literally preached at me for months. Maybe it was because they knew only too well how easy it was to become a product of this neighborhood, with its culture of crime. After a while I began to buy into some of this honesty talk – at least in the evenings. Each morning I went out and stole cars, but in the evenings I was honest! Sometimes they mentioned to me the fact that cars kept being stolen in the area; they said they would love to catch the person who was doing it. I *was* that person, but they didn't know it.

But after slowly wearing down my resolve with their talk over many months, Keith and Johnny actually convinced me to take the test required to become a New Orleans police officer. I simply laughed when they first suggested it. I wasn't interested in the Police

Department or being a cop. In fact, everyone I knew told me that the cops were as crooked as the criminals. You could not find one person in Hollygrove who liked cops – no one. I truly believed at that time that Keith and Johnny were probably the only honest cops in the Department. Nevertheless, something within me rose to the challenge and I thought about it a lot. Eventually, I went to speak to Grandma about it and, when she had finished laughing hysterically, she also agreed that I should give it a try.

I'd always been a naturally smart person – so Grandma always told me, as well as a number of crooks – and I was particularly good at figuring people out. I could tell you pretty accurately, just by looking at someone walking down the street, based on observation alone, what they did for a living. It became a kind of game to me. But this natural intuitiveness would become an important asset to me later. When finally I took the police test, I passed the written exam easily. I also passed the physical fitness challenge without any problem. In fact, the tester was astounded at my athletic ability. It didn't surprise me, of course. I was a good crook and good crooks learn to run fast before they begin stealing.

I was fine with these first two tests. My main worry was the impending psychological test. Here, an officer interrogated you thoroughly and the line of questioning was designed to catch you out. Its purpose was to weed out of the selection process all the mental cases and all those with criminal tendencies and a weakness for lying. Guess what happened? I passed. The psychologist asked me dumb questions like, "Have you ever stolen anything?" I looked at him like he was nuts. Who in their right mind would answer yes? "No," I answered flatly. I was good at lying. In my own way, I convinced myself I was genuinely telling the truth. I had given up auto theft and all other criminal activities just fifteen minutes *before* entering the room! In my mind, I interpreted the question to mean, "Do you *intend* to steal anything?" – and I didn't.

At this point, I still wasn't totally sold on wanting to become a police officer. I had taken the test more as a challenge, just to see how far I could get. But once the testing was done, Grandma and I talked more about it and I began to consider it as a serious opportunity to get myself out of the ghetto. In due course I received the news: I had passed all the tests and was being offered a place to train to be a police officer!

I had three months to make up my mind. In order to assist my decision-making, I started reading the Bible every night – on strict orders from Grandma. As I read, I really believed what God was saying. I felt that, deep down, there might be some hope for someone like me. Maybe I had become a crook because I didn't know any other way. I knew there must be some chance of reforming me, if only for the reason that every time I committed a crime, I felt terrible remorse afterwards. Everywhere in our house were pictures, trinkets, sayings from the Bible, statues of Jesus, crosses, angels... anything and everything associated with God. I loved Grandma deeply and knew how religious she was. I also knew she had no idea about my stealing. I had successfully pulled the wool over her eyes for a long time. For her sake as much as my own, I made up my mind I was going to become a police officer. This was my chance to make a different life.

So it was that a few months later I began to attend the prestigious New Orleans Police Academy. And prestigious it was. The instructors at the Academy were passionate about their training. They covered every conceivable situation an officer might come up against. I remember my instructor, Sergeant Duke, was a proficient, respectable officer who drilled us thoroughly.

As soon you enter the Academy as a trainee you are issued a uniform (minus any weapon, of course) and are expected to wear it when traveling to and from work. This caused an immediate problem for me living in Hollygrove. All my friends abandoned me as soon as they heard I was a police trainee and saw me wearing that uniform. Many of the drug dealers I knew were especially nervous about ever having known me, and I knew I needed to move out of Hollygrove quickly. I was not one of the criminals there any more. Grandma was happy for me. I don't think she ever doubted I could become a police officer, only my desire to do it. I moved out of Hollygrove into a nice area and looked forward to what the future might hold.

I graduated from the Police Academy in 1978 with honors. There are only three honors given to trainees in each class and I earned one of them – the physical fitness award, given to the student who demonstrates an overall superior performance in running, climbing and general fitness. These are the main tools of police officers, vital to their ability to apprehend criminals. This particular award was especially coveted by trainees because it meant the possibility of choice assignments and promotions in the future, such as joining a SWAT team or tactical unit.

After graduation I was given my first work placement. Guess where the Department decided to place this award-winning police officer? I was assigned to the Fifth District, which encompassed New Orleans' worst housing areas. These weren't just ghettos, they were super-ghettos. I guess they thought my physical skills could be put to good use catching robbers. It didn't matter to me – I had no choice anyway.

* * *

My first day on the job was extremely moving. I awoke that morning, ironed my uniform and polished my shoes. Before leaving the house, I walked over to my full-sized bedroom mirror to see how I appeared. I was clean as a slate and sharp as a tack. I walked to my car, drove to the Police Precinct and reported for duty. There I was introduced to the man who would be my partner – a seasoned veteran – and we got to know each other a little as we patrolled the streets of New Orleans in our police cruiser. He told me about his many years on the job, the experiences he had been through, and his hopes for retirement in just a few years' time.

Our patrols and conversations continued much the same for several otherwise uneventful days. Then one day a call came over the radio instructing us to proceed to a nearby location to investigate a rape. We hurried to the scene with emergency lights on and the siren blasting. As we got out of the car we saw a young girl, around eleven or twelve years old, standing next to a vacant building. She came up to us, obviously shocked and distraught. We spoke to her and she told us in detail about how she was walking to school when an adult male approached her, forced her to enter the vacant building and then raped her. Her eyes welled with tears as she recounted her ordeal and I noticed her clothing was still in disarray. She walked, clearly still in physical discomfort from the attack, and showed us where the crime had taken place. We quickly called our supervisor to the scene as well as a forensic team to assist us. My head was reeling. I wondered how a thirty-five-year-old adult could forcefully rape a child. She was completely traumatized. We attempted to comfort her and a short while later her parents arrived to take her home.

If I'd had any doubts before, I realized now that this new vocation of mine would lead me into many horrible circumstances. There and then I had to write a report about the crime which would later be filed. As I tried to put pen to paper I was shaking badly. I glanced up to see my veteran partner looking at me with a mixture of compassion and resignation. He leaned over as I wrote and whispered softly, "You must deal with this as though it doesn't exist. You cannot be attached or close to the victim. Report what you observed without sorrow, tears or pain." I looked at him, wondering how it was possible to detach oneself from such trauma. "The rape has occurred and there is nothing you can do about it," he continued. "The best we can do for that little girl, Robert, is to record everything carefully, so we can apprehend the perpetrator."

Right then I felt as traumatized as the victim. I felt her pain and had compassion for her. I didn't doubt that my partner was a compassionate man too, but he remained cool and free of tension. He had investigated many rapes and had hardened himself to the harshness of reality. I was just a rookie, totally unprepared for this. Eventually, we finished our part of the investigation at the crime scene and left. "Time for lunch," my partner commented. He ate lunch, but I didn't touch a thing. How could I eat after that ordeal? For the rest of the day the incident constantly played on my mind. That evening when I returned home I sat down and thought things through. "This is the profession I've chosen," I told myself. "I must deal with this, because it *will* happen again."

I was right, of course. Many of the upcoming days and weeks were difficult. I saw many dreadful events which had a marked effect on me. Sometimes I was filled with fear and at other times I just felt sick. Often, I simply felt unhappy. As time passed, however, just as my partner said it would, the challenge of dealing with victims and the crimes perpetrated on them became easier to cope with. I began to harden myself to reality, just as he had done.

Once, when I was working alone, the police dispatcher instructed me to investigate a call in a seedy part of the Industrial Canal. It appeared to be a regular, domestic-type call. I arrived, parked my vehicle and proceeded to get out of it. As I exited the cruiser, someone (or more than one person) started shooting at me. I caught only a glimpse of him and the flash of his weapon. Immediately I jumped on the hood of my car, rolled across it to take cover and began returning fire. We exchanged shots with each other as if we were in a Western shootout. Eventually the culprit or culprits fled the scene. I didn't know if I'd shot anyone during this chaos, but I was happy none of the bullets had hit me.

After this commotion was over, ten or twelve police cars arrived at the scene. I was taken to hospital to be examined because I had hit my neck and back on a fire hydrant I hadn't seen as I'd rolled over my cruiser and landed on the other side. But after a brief examination and a few tests I was deemed fit to return to duty. Despite incidents like these, which often seemed surreal at the time, I flourished in the Fifth District. I arrested robbers, thieves, rapists and all kinds of criminals. "What a job," I thought. "A former criminal, now a police officer."

I want to reveal a number of things about the New Orleans Police Department which occurred during my tenure there. These are things I've been told repeatedly by former and current officers not to say, but I feel I need to say them in order to come clean with everything. There were a lot of corrupt cops in New Orleans; bad cops, dishonest to the core. Some cops I met actually sold drugs from their squad cars. They took money from arrestees. They pilfered drugs from dealers in order to sell on. I knew two cops who regularly smoked dope in their squad car. I saw all these things and realized that being a cop in New Orleans wasn't all about honesty. Yet, the very reason I had joined was a desire to become honest, honorable, and to "do the right thing", as Grandma would say.

The corruption was so bad that it found its way up into the officers' corps. Captains and Lieutenants were as corrupt as their minions. In practice, this meant that there was no proper supervision over the regular cops. Cops were having sex on the job, even with other cops. In later years the Federal Government, realizing the depth of the corruption in New Orleans, developed a special Federal Task Force to investigate the Police Department. But if you think this stopped the corruption, guess again.

Perhaps the lowest point came when the New Orleans Police Department was discovered to have a serial killer in its midst. The killer was one of its officers – a female officer, no less. Around the same time, police officers were killing witnesses who lodged complaints against them. In short, the Department was a cesspool of dishonesty and corruption. In my opinion, a visitor to the city was more likely to be attacked by a police officer than a criminal. There were some noble and dedicated officers on the force, but their devotion to the populace was overshadowed by so much corruption. I wish I could have had the benefit of belonging to that particular group of men – but unfortunately I didn't.

In 1978, I met a nurse called Candace. We eventually built a life together. I often went home to Candace and shared with her the things I witnessed in the Department. She was rightly shocked and appalled because she'd had a good upbringing and had been taught the value of honesty and dignity. She had become a nurse because she had a passion for helping others. It was these qualities that caused me to fall in love with her. When I told her about the corruption in the force, she simply admonished me to *do the right thing*, just like Grandma. I really wanted to. But little did she know, or I for that matter, that one day I would join the club along with all the other bad cops.

Chapter 3

Crossing the Line

In the police force there is such a thing as a code of silence. If you witnessed another officer beating someone, protocol dictated that you didn't say anything. You couldn't. If you did, you were immediately "branded". To be "branded" was a term officers used to mark you out as a rat. If that happened, you immediately lost the trust and support of your colleagues and this would manifest itself in very real ways. If, for example, a "branded" officer arrived at the scene of a robbery in progress and called the dispatcher for back-up, instead of officers arriving in two minutes, they might turn up in eight or ten. That is a tremendous amount of time for an officer to be alone on a "hot call". In other words, rats were made to be exposed and vulnerable, to increase their chances of being injured.

The Department was infested with crooks. In many ways there was little difference between a bad cop and a crook living in Hollygrove. One had a gun, the other had a gun and a badge. One committed crime by taking what they wanted, the other took it by manipulating and abusing their authority. What was the difference, really? If I was forced to give an estimate, I would say that seven out of ten officers in the Department were corrupt to one degree or another. But I knew I was powerless to do anything about it. I didn't want to be branded. I certainly didn't want other officers deliberately making my job more difficult than it was already. I decided to keep my mouth shut and get on with it. I succeeded for a while, until one day when, under pressure from a colleague, I crossed a line I would never be able to come back from.

On that particular day, during roll-call, I was paired with a cop I had never worked with before, because my regular partner was on sick leave. While on patrol, we observed a car speeding down the street. In it were two females. We turned around and gave chase. Eventually we pulled them over, with sirens wailing, and approached their vehicle. My partner demanded to see the driver's license so that he could issue a citation. He proceeded to write the ticket, but halfway through he paused, looked up, and said matter-of-factly, "Would you girls like to make a deal?" I frowned and wondered what he was talking about.

"What kind of deal?" the driver inquired.

"Sex for the citations," came the flat reply.

Both the young women were shocked. "No way!" they retorted. At that my partner simply responded, "OK, you are both under arrest."

"What for?" the girls protested.

"I'll think of something," he growled back at them.

He hustled them out of their car and placed them in the back of our squad car while they pleaded with him to stop. We all got in the vehicle and he began reciting a number of charges that he would file against them, informing them that they would be far better off cooperating with him. He continued to tell them how much trouble they would be in until, eventually, both women agreed to have sex with him.

What was I doing whilst this terrible scene unfolded? Honestly, I did nothing. I just watched events play out while a terrible sinking feeling gripped my gut. For one thing, I was the junior officer there and we always deferred to a senior officer's authority. I could have protested, but I chose not to. Secondly, I did not want to be branded and break the unspoken protocol of corruption. I kept my mouth shut, but then I was dragged even deeper into this mess.

"Which one do you want?" my partner asked casually.

"Neither one," I said nervously.

"What?" he responded. "Take a careful look at these girls. Have you ever seen ladies this fine, this beautiful?"

"You're crazy," I said. "Besides, where are we going to take them?"

He asked me to step out of the car so he could talk to me privately. We had already learned that they were models visiting from Boston and clearly he didn't want to let go of this opportunity. He worked hard on me and repeated over and over how beautiful these girls were and what great bodies they had. As I stood on the sidewalk one of the girls in the car was looking at me. She was quite beautiful and bit by bit I began to give in. I began to justify the crime I was about to commit. "Maybe it wouldn't hurt this one time," I persuaded myself. My head began to swim with desire and anticipation. Now all I could think about was my own pleasure. He had talked me into it and now there was no going back.

We drove to a desolate part of town, which was not hard to find, and had sex. Then we drove them back to their vehicle. When we arrived I fully expected that we would drop them off at their car and that would be it. I was astonished when my partner then proceeded to give them three citations. The girls were just as shocked as I was. They protested that they had "done the deal", so why was he issuing citations? Unrepentant, this corrupt officer threatened them again with more serious charges and possible jail time, so they decided to take the citations and leave things as they were. Back in our patrol car, my temporary partner told me why he'd issued the tickets.

"You always have to cover your butt in case they file charges with the Internal Affairs Division," he cautioned. "It would look bad if we pulled them over for speeding and then didn't issue a ticket."

"That's cold," I replied.

"Better to be cold than stupid," he said.

We finished the rest of our shift by congratulating each other on this wicked deed, but at the end of the day I had to return home and face Candace. Every day when I came home we talked about the day's events and shared what had happened. Of course, I neglected to mention my sordid betrayal.

The agreement I struck with my partner that day marked one

of the *worst and most despicable days of my life*. The choice I made that day is the reason why I am sharing this story. It is the reason why my life went down into the abyss. The moment I became complicit to my partner's crime and decided to participate in this wrongdoing, I dishonored my Grandma, my sisters, my mother – in fact, every female on the planet. That really meant something to me. Although I was a reluctant police officer to begin with, my job on the New Orleans Police Force had become special to me. But now? Now I was a crook again. The same crook that I was back in Hollygrove, but wearing different clothes. The trust given to me by the citizens of New Orleans had been grossly violated.

Even after all these years, I wish I could find those women and apologize to them. Although I have stated from the beginning that before becoming a police officer I was a thief and a crook, even the crooks in Hollygrove had a code of ethics. We were never disrespectful towards women, never degraded them. We wouldn't steal a woman's car if we knew that she was living alone. At home, the females in our household were always given respect. I love my three sisters and have always respected them. They ate first, took showers first and always got offered the last food in the pot before the boys did. None of us boys were allowed to put our hands on the girls – not for any reason, at any time.

My Grandma had always taught me to do the right thing. The preacher at church on Sundays always said to do the right thing. But in the war that took place in my mind, Satan won. The truth is, whether we like it or not, we are all in a spiritual battle. It's about making the right choices and doing the right thing, even when no one is looking. Satan won because I let him win. I thought I was so high and mighty wearing my police badge and catching criminals, but the fact was, I was a crook. Not only had I helped to violate two innocent people, but my partner and I had made them agree to it. I had prided myself on not hanging around with the bad cops at the Precinct. Now I was a bad cop.

I was happy to see my regular partner, Andrew, return from sick leave the next day. I didn't dare tell him about the previous night's events. He was a good cop. Andrew and I had an honorable tour that evening, but just a week later we were separated due to shift rotations. I was assigned to work the evening shift with another partner for one month.

Since I was now an experienced cop with some time under my belt, I was assigned to patrol the notorious Canal area. Actually it was called the Industrial Canal, but it was referred to in New Orleans simply as "Canal" – an area with a very high concentration of criminals. As my partner and I patrolled the area one night, a call came over the radio regarding a possible stolen car in the area. We went to the location in question but saw nothing. Then, as we were parked on the corner, a car closely matching the description zoomed past us. We proceeded to chase the vehicle and I knew instinctively this was likely the stolen car we were looking for. I called for back-up to assist us with the chase.

Eventually, we stopped the stolen vehicle and were surprised to see a female driver. Her name was Valerie. I arrested her and we transported her to central lockup. Once she had been admitted I took her into one of the interrogation cells – a small windowless room, except for a tiny peephole in the door. Valerie was a good-looking lady around my age. As I filled out the arrest report and proceeded to interrogate her about the stolen car, I could see she was very afraid. She knew she was looking at some extremely serious felony charges, as well as numerous citations. An idea quickly formed in my head.

Once you cross a line, it's very difficult to come back. When you violate your conscience you try to find reasons and excuses to justify your actions. Ever since the encounter with the two models months earlier, I had come to accept the fact that I was crooked, just like the majority of my colleagues. I had grown comfortable with the idea, grown used to hiding my corruption from Candace, though I loved her. Any time a corrupt cop can take advantage of a situation, most times he will do it. And here, sitting in front of me, was a woman who was clearly scared of what would happen to her. I fully intended to take advantage of Valerie's vulnerability.

Echoing the words of my fellow officer, I asked her if she wanted to "make a deal". At first she didn't know what I was speaking about, so I told her bluntly: if she would give me sex, I would try to have some of the charges against her dropped. She told me she didn't want to do that. I ignored her, kept talking and eventually convinced her that this was in her best interests. After some time, she agreed to do as I requested. It was through pure intimidation that Valerie submitted. If I had been a good officer I wouldn't even have suggested such a wicked thing. We completed the act and I got Valerie's home number, informing her that I would try to get some of the charges dropped.

Again, I found myself practicing crooked justice. Once you start down that road, it's hard to stop. I didn't give a thought to being faithful to Candace, I was only concerned about my own physical gratification. I was supposed to be out on the streets looking for criminals, tackling crime, but the crime was right there within me. Soon after the act was finished, I felt ashamed, just as I had felt with those other two ladies. Looking back, I realize that I had tuned out any thoughts of my Grandma or what I knew of God. Thinking of either would only have brought condemnation to my mind. After committing this offence, I went home that night as normal, kissed Candace and went to bed, crookedly. A crook in the daytime is still a crook when he's asleep.

Little did I know, Valerie had reported the entire incident to the Department of Internal Affairs. She told them everything. Ignorant of this fact, I called Valerie often and asked to see her. I didn't know she had agreed to have her telephone wired to record all our conversations. For some strange reason I latched onto her more than any other woman. Other crooked cops had told me never to hit on the same victim twice. I didn't listen to their advice. Each time I spoke to her, there was an audiotape made of everything we discussed. After about a week of talking, I suggested Valerie and I meet and she agreed. I imagine Internal Affairs also thought we should meet. The sting was set up to arrest me as soon as Valerie and I met. I arrived at the meeting place a few minutes ahead of her and waited.

This was October 1979. I was twenty-four years old. I parked my brand-new 1979 Pontiac Trans Am, clean as a whistle and fast as a bullet, in the agreed spot and sat. Around five officers from Internal Affairs had already staked out the site before I arrived. They had every conceivable exit blocked. I listened to the radio until Valerie pulled up behind me. I thought it a little strange that she parked behind me instead of pulling alongside, but quickly dismissed the thought. Valerie was wearing a wire to record our conversation. She walked to the car and spoke to me. I told her to get in so we could take a ride; but she didn't get in, she just kept talking to me through the door.

I listened for a bit longer and asked her again to get in the car. She didn't move. Now my police training kicked in. Something was wrong. I glanced in the rear-view mirror and caught sight of a man running toward my car. At the same instant, in my peripheral vision I saw another man approaching my car, just off to the right, and then a third man. Valerie backed away. I hit the accelerator on that Trans Am and sped away, my mind racing, trying to figure out what was going on. I was the police. I don't run; other people run! Through my rear-view mirror I saw at least five men running to their cars to chase me. I racked my brain to find a reason why this was happening. Had some drug dealer I'd taken down arranged a hit on me? Who had I crossed who now wanted revenge?

The Fifth District Police Station was only two or three minutes away. I figured I should get there, and quick. I pushed the Trans Am as hard as I could, until I was traveling at 100 mph down a residential street, but my pursuers were still chasing me, even two blocks from the Police Station. "Once I get to the Station, they won't dare follow me in," I thought. But as I swung into the parking lot, tires screaming, I could see they were still following. I slammed on the brakes, grabbed my gun from the glove compartment, and tumbled out of the car preparing myself to do battle.

It was then that one of my supervisors came out of the Police Station looking confused. I looked over at him and yelled, "Sergeant, somebody's chasing me!" He called back to me, "I just heard the order to apprehend you broadcast on the police radio." The men

I prayed for some miracle,
but deep down inside I
knew I was a dead man.

Chapter 4

No Way Out

After a short journey we arrived at the Internal Affairs office, where I was booked. I spotted an officer who used to work in the Fifth District, who had transferred to the Internal Affairs Division. Before his move we had been good friends. He was a fellow crook. "Surely," I thought to myself, "he will tell me what is going on." He didn't. He didn't say a word. At this time, I had not connected any of these events to Valerie and my crime. I was genuinely puzzled by what was taking place. I was interrogated for about an hour and I just kept thinking, "I wonder what's happened to her?" It wasn't until later that night that I was told the reason for my arrest – Valerie – and then everything began to make disturbing sense.

Sitting there in jail, I was gripped by cold, sheer terror. I had never felt such fear in my whole life. Looking back, I can appreciate how scared some of our victims must have felt, knowing that their fate was in someone else's hands and they could do little about it. I didn't know how or if I was going to be able to get out of this. Two hours after my arrest my crime was all over the local news and suddenly everyone knew my name. I was allowed to make one phone call, like all other prisoners. I called Candace. She had already heard about my arrest on the news and was making arrangements to come and get me out.

I was being kept in a special holding cell for safety reasons. The other prisoners were salivating to get their hands on me. A police officer cannot live amongst the general prison population, because someone is bound to kill you. I had already spotted one prisoner I had put in there myself about a month previously, for committing assault and battery on his wife. Imagine how much he would have loved to make my acquaintance again. Crooks, thieves, robbers, rapists and murderers were all around me. They couldn't intimidate me physically, I knew. Hardly anyone could take me on man to man, because I was very fit and I worked out a lot with weights. I was buffed; I could take care of myself. No, my biggest fear wasn't these monsters, but facing Candace. All I could think of was Grandma saying to me, "I told you, son, to do the right thing!"

Eventually Candace arrived and she bonded me out of jail. As we drove back home there was absolute silence in the car. For thirty minutes neither of us spoke a word. When we arrived home at least fifteen of our neighbors were milling around outside. "Hell," I thought, "no one ever stands outside in this neighborhood." We got out of the car to go inside and endured the neighbors staring and whispering to one another. That didn't bother me at all, but it bothered me that I was humiliating Candace. I could tell she was deeply embarrassed. She walked into the house with me following her like a wimp. As soon as we had closed the door, she fainted – she literally collapsed. It took me a good few minutes to revive her and gently place her on the sofa. When she opened her eyes and looked at me she simply said, "Robert, I will fight for you in front of anyone, any time." As I began to say something she stopped me and said, "I'm going to bed now. We will talk in the morning."

As she retired, I sat on our patio looking up at the stars and suddenly saw a falling star. "How appropriate," I thought. I sat there feeling nothing. I wasn't hungry, thirsty or sleepy. I cannot begin to tell you the sense of shame I felt, the shame I knew I had brought upon my family – not just Candace, but my mother, brothers and sisters. Grandma had passed away some two years before that day. I was relieved that she, of all people, would be spared the humiliation. At this moment I thought of my father. For the past twenty-four years I had never given him a thought. In truth, I hated his guts. I despised him for running out on his family and not being around to guide us properly. Maybe, if he had been in my life, this wouldn't have happened. "Who is this man?" I asked myself time and time again. "Where is he?" "How can God allow this to happen to a bunch of innocent kids?" I had so many unanswered questions. I was consumed with remorse on a scale I'd never experienced before – tormented, devastated by my own stupidity. All the feelings of terror I had caused my victims were now being visited upon me.

The sound of a police siren interrupted my thoughts and from the patio I could see the police cruiser in the distance with its emergency lights on. The cops were pulling someone over a couple of blocks away. Seeing it made me feel sick. "Is it a good cop or a bad cop?" I asked myself. "Is he about to violate that citizen? Maybe I should yell out to him, 'Don't do that! Don't violate that woman!'" But as I pondered these words, I knew my name was all over the city. No cop would do anything wrong tonight, I figured.

I went inside, sat on the sofa, turned off the lights and cried. Tears streamed down my cheeks for the next hour. When my glands could no longer manufacture liquid tears, I cried in my soul. This was the worst cry – my spiritual self turned inside out. Somehow, I fell asleep. I was awakened at 5 a.m. by Candace, coming to lie down next to me. She simply said, "I love you." In a few minutes, she was fast asleep again. I looked at the dried tear-trails tracing her cheeks and at that moment I realized just how much she loved me. As I lay there, the room still shrouded with darkness, I thought I saw another falling star, but realized it must be headlights reflecting from the nearby highway.

As the day dawned I knew it would be a day of reckoning. Candace and I sat at the kitchen table and stared at each other. She told me we needed to find a good attorney. As I tried to explain how I had gotten myself into this mess, she interrupted me. "Robert, I don't want to hear anything about this. I simply want to find an attorney, fight this, and see if we have a future together." Not once did Candace ask me if I had committed the crime I was accused of. I guess she already knew the answer to that because of my silence in the car. During the entire time Candace and I were together, she never ever questioned me. It was a strange love she had for me, unlike any I've seen.

We attempted to find an attorney we could afford, but every one of them had heard about my case already and demanded huge fees. At a hearing one week later, I finally asked the court to appoint an attorney to represent me. My trial was set for January 1980. I thought to myself, "How can I go on living with this torture for another three months before the trial?" In the meantime, many crooked cops came to my house to show their support. It is amazing how cops stick together, even if they are wrong. Candace went to work at the hospital each day while I sat around the house, day and night, crying and sulking about my situation. I was aware of the acute embarrassment Candace was going through at work each day, with her co-workers looking at her strangely and conducting whispered conversations in the corridors. "Oh, Robert, what have you done?" I said to myself repeatedly.

A few days later I had to attend court for a pre-trial hearing. As I was sitting in the courtroom, waiting for the judge to call me up, a trial was in progress. A nineteen-year-old black male was being tried for a murder he had committed a few months earlier. The verdict was "Guilty" and the judge sentenced him on the spot. He was given life in Angola prison. The young man hung his head, all hope evaporating as he realized his life was over. I thought about the sentence and what his life would look like from this moment on. I had a sinking feeling about my own destiny.

A few seconds later, as they were leading that young man out of court, he turned around and tried to run. Everyone in the court started screaming due to this surprise. He wasn't handcuffed, so he tried to jump over the swinging door separating the court proper from the visitors' seating. As he jumped he caught his foot and fell, and the sheriffs quickly subdued him. As they began to take him away, I looked over at his crying family and thought to myself, "God Almighty, I'm in a lot of trouble." I was looking at thirty years in prison – in Angola prison, like this young man. Angola is the state prison system for Louisiana's hard-core prisoners and has been the subject of many documentaries on television. Being a former cop, I knew that upon my conviction and transfer to Angola, I could easily be dead within twenty-four hours. I was not prepared to die, but it seemed a very real and imminent possibility. As my trial date was set by the judge, I left that court feeling nothing but doom.

When I returned home, I prayed for some miracle, but deep down inside I knew I was a dead man. It was then that I knew I had a decision to make. I was set on a course that would result in either incarceration for pretty much the rest of my life or a sudden, horrible death at the hands of some psychotic inmate. I couldn't get off this path I had set for myself. I could do nothing about it... or so I thought at first.

But then an idea began to form in my head. What if I ran? What if I became a fugitive from justice? This disgraced police officer was about to make another terrible decision – to run, as fast and as far as I could to avoid my certain fate. I knew full well that every police officer in New Orleans would be hunting me down. I knew that the FBI and the US Marshal's Office would join in the search. "But, I have a good chance," I reasoned. I had valuable training and an insider's knowledge of police tactics and procedures.

Gradually I embraced the idea that I would run and hide, evade capture. I had been a criminal living on my wits back in Hollygrove. Now I was a criminal with police training and knowledge. Surely, such a person could elude capture. If I couldn't do it, then no one could. I had always relished a challenge. This would be my greatest yet. I resolved to do battle with the system, me against the establishment. I had it all worked out in my mind by the time Candace returned home from work that day. Logically, I had concluded that I must go it alone, not drag her into this, and that could only mean one thing.

"I want to split up," I informed her. "Go and stay at your sister's place for a while, and after I'm gone I want you to start a new life with another man."

I was too scared to tell her exactly what I planned to do. "I can't ask her to come with me," I thought. I just wanted her to go, to be safe. After I finished my speech she just looked at me. She had already guessed what I was planning.

"Robert," she said, "I love you very much. I sense you are either going to commit suicide or run. Knowing you, you have probably decided to run."

I stared at her, not knowing what to say.

"If you are going to run," she continued, "I will run with you, and if you run without me, I will commit suicide."

"God," I thought, "I've just sentenced her to death! I mean, if she stays behind while I run, she'll end her own life. But if she runs with me she might die too. What if we end up in a shoot-out someplace?"

Rather than leave her behind and not know what would become of her, I agreed to take her with me. From that moment on things changed dramatically. We knew we had to leave everything behind us. There was no more talk about the trial, attorneys, rent, furniture, cars, bills, her job, friends or family. We agreed that everything would have to be forsaken if this was going to work. More than that, we knew we were giving up our very identities. It also meant that Candace would become a fugitive, just like me, but she was prepared to do it. She quit her job the next day.

Two weeks before my trial date, I had figured out all the logistics associated with becoming a fugitive. I sold everything we owned except one car and we had about $3,000 dollars in cash. One morning we decided that "this was the day" and it was time to make our move. We took a few things with us and closed our apartment door for the last time. We drove to Baton Rouge, ditched the car and our identification at the airport, then caught a cab back to downtown Baton Rouge near the bus station. I wanted our hunters to think we had taken a flight somewhere. That journey was very surreal for us. We knew there was no turning back. This would be my first logistical move in evading capture – the first of many such moves that would keep me running scared for the next twenty-two years.

After all I had been through,
I felt that no reasoning or
logic could defend a God.

Chapter 5

Toronto, Canada – on the Run

My next logistical move was to get out of the United States. Candace and I arrived in Canada using fake identification cards I had manufactured before we left home. It cost me just $500 to get the equipment needed to make the IDs. I'm not going to divulge what equipment I used, though, as I don't want to help another foolish person do what I did. Needless to say, the equipment was easily available.

We arrived in Toronto and spent the first night in a seedy hotel. A few days later, I rented an apartment near Bloor Street in downtown Toronto. I used more fake documents to show that Candace and I were gainfully employed in order to secure the lease. It was a small studio apartment, ideal for our journey. I had chosen it for security reasons: the apartment had one large window to the front, facing the only way to get in, and another large window at the rear, facing a wooded area. The front window allowed me to see anyone who might approach the apartment and the rear window provided a quick escape route into the cover of the woods. I purchased a shortwave radio and constantly monitored all police activity in the area. I told Candace I had a plan for making some money, but didn't divulge the details to her.

Upon our arrival in the area, Candace had noticed a couple of people selling flowers on a street corner. She asked around and found out it was a cash job. People were making $40 to $60 a day selling roses. She had hit upon a great way to make some quick cash. One of the first things I'd told her was that we needed to find a job with no paper trail and no income tax deductions. She had followed my instructions meticulously and I was pleased. I knew we would need to rely on our wits and live carefully in order to get through this. I showed her as many tricks as I could to help us survive this journey.

My only worry was that Candace missed her sister very much. They would always see each other or speak on the phone when we were back in Louisiana and they were very close. Her relationship with God was important to her as well. Though she had made some very difficult, perhaps questionable decisions about sticking with me, her faith in God remained constant. I think she believed that he would see us through this, one way or another.

As far as God was concerned, I had gone in the opposite direction. I didn't care about him at this point. I had decided I was an atheist. After all I had been through, I felt that no reasoning or logic could defend a God. In my spare time, I would go to the library and read books on atheistic philosophy. I deduced from my research that God was non-existent and the Bible nothing more than a novel written by some smart scribes. I reasoned that the scribes were probably crooks, like me, who had a motive for pulling the wool over our eyes. I was my own god, I decided.

For a few days I searched around the seedy backstreets of Toronto to try and find a chop shop. Every city has one: a place that buys stolen car parts. While Candace sold flowers on the street corner, I returned to my first ever trade: stealing cars, stripping them for the parts and selling them on. I was pleased to discover that cars were easier to steal in Canada than the US because Canadians were naive about crime. In general, the crime rate was very low, and four out of five cars still had their keys in the ignition. I rented a storage facility large enough to park a car, and four hours later that car was a shell – I mean, stripped to the bone. Business was great and Candace and I flourished. I made more money than ever before and I developed friendships with many local crooks. Apart from stealing cars, I had no need to commit other crimes.

As the days went by, Candace no longer needed to sell roses, since my car-stealing business was thriving. We had a nice apartment, we ate well and we paid the bills. Every evening, we watched television with a special emphasis on the news. Every time the news came on, we were afraid I might be the subject of it. In fact, I felt nervous and slightly nauseous whenever news time approached. My status as a fugitive took a toll on Candace too. She coped with it as best she could, but I knew it was a big leap from living in New Orleans to living in Canada. It was difficult for her to go from being a professional, well-paid nurse to selling flowers on a street corner. Each night I looked at her as she slept. Yes, she was physically in bed with me, but her mind, I knew, was in Louisiana. We talked about our life together often. We wondered what we would do if we ever decided to have children, since we didn't have any legitimate identification. What if one of us needed to go to the hospital at some point? Could we ever drive a vehicle again?

Every night Candace would spend time reading her Bible. Sometimes she would ask me to read with her, but I always made an excuse to get out of it. Though I had decided I no longer believed in God, I never said anything to her about these nightly sessions. "If her faith is helping her get through these harsh conditions," I thought, "then let her do it." I knew she needed some source of strength. I found it much more difficult to tolerate, though, when she began buying crosses and other religious junk and placing them on the walls. I was disgusted about this. She put a cross on the wall, directly above the television, and as I watched the commercials, my eyes would constantly be drawn to it. I hated God and anything associated with him. Then she started bringing home religious pamphlets and positioning them strategically around the place where I would, she hoped, find and read them. Everywhere I looked, I observed all this garbage. I desperately wished to tell her this God stuff was foolishness, but I never let on to Candace that I was a hard-core atheist. I think she would have left me immediately if she'd known.

On another occasion, I came home and noticed Candace had placed a mat outside the front door with "Jesus Loves You" written on it. I stopped, looked at the mat and sighed. Then, I happily stomped on it in defiance and disgust. As I entered the apartment, she was watching a program with some stupid preacher talking about love. I went over to greet her, but straight away went into the bedroom. As I laid on the bed, I didn't know which was worse: being on the run as a fugitive or living with Jesus.

I began to feel like I was being pursued by Jesus, not just the police. One day as I left our apartment to "go to work", I stopped to pick up some breakfast at a local diner. As I was sitting at the table, a gentleman walked in passing out Christian pamphlets. I don't know what made him do it, but this guy came directly to my table and attempted to hand one to me. I told him proudly that I didn't believe in God. After I said this, he just sat across the table from me without asking if it was OK. This really annoyed me and I was about to speak to him about his rude behavior, but I didn't want to attract attention or cause a scene, so quickly decided not to.

As I suspected, he was thinking that he could convince me that God existed. For the next twenty minutes he sat and talked at me, going over and over the Bible and its teachings. During the entire length of this "sermon" I said nothing. I just nodded occasionally, acting as if I was interested. When I sensed he was nearly finished with this God talk, I asked him a question. I said I wanted to see his Bible and he happily obliged. I flipped through the pages, found a particular passage and asked if he would give me his opinion on it. "Of course," he replied. I handed the Bible back and asked him to read two paragraphs from the book of Genesis.

Then I pointed out to him the contradictions in the text. He looked puzzled, took his reading glasses out of his suit pocket to study the verses more closely and stumbled over his words as he tried to give me an explanation. As he was re-reading the paragraphs, I stood up to leave. I just walked away while he was still trying to figure out what to say to me. "What an ignorant fool," I thought. I couldn't understand why, if God was real, he always sent emissaries like these to represent him – people who easily got tripped up and confused concerning the Bible.

The way I saw it, if you called yourself an automobile mechanic, then you should know everything there is to know about cars. You can't call yourself a mechanic if all you can do is complete an oil change. Surely it's the same for Christians? If you are going to call yourself one, then you should know your subject inside out! I had no time for these weak-minded individuals. As I went to work, I enjoyed laughing at that fool in the diner.

In my line of "work", there was only one type of vehicle I could not steal. It wasn't because I couldn't break it or hotwire it, I simply refused to steal it. It was any vehicle that had a cross dangling from the rear-view mirror, or a Bible on the dashboard, or religious bumper stickers. I honestly believed that stealing such cars would jinx me and bring me bad luck. Instead, as an act of defiance to God, I "keyed" them, dragging a small pocket-knife down the side from headlight to taillight. Afterwards I mockingly asked, "Why didn't your God stop me?"

* * *

In January 1980, it was cold in Canada – bitterly cold. In Toronto, it snows quite a bit in the first months of each year – so different from New Orleans – and yet it was a beautiful city. I watched many of the city's hockey games and became quite fond of this unusual sport. Back in Louisiana, we didn't have hockey.

Life carried on much as it had for the past year, until one day when I returned home from work. As I opened the apartment door, my senses perceived something was out of place. Something was wrong. What was it? My senses were not giving off danger signals, but fear signals – a type of fear of abandonment. As I walked around the apartment, I noticed that it was unusually clean. My fear led me to the closet. All Candace's clothes were gone. Instantly I knew: "She's left me." All her belongings had disappeared; there was no trace of her left.

I could only assume she had returned home to Louisiana. I sank to the floor, looking at the empty closet in front of me, and cried. After a while I got up and searched around to see if she had left any kind of note. "Surely there must be a note," I thought, but there was nothing. "Oh, Candace," I cried, "I love you so much!" It was as though the very last piece of Louisiana, of home, that I had clung onto had been ripped away from me. I was truly alone. "Candace," I cried again, "I'm so sorry." Part of me wished she had never left New Orleans with me. At least now I wouldn't be feeling this pain and devastation.

I never saw Candace again. Ultimately, I didn't blame her for leaving. Everything about this new life was scary and unpredictable and she missed her sister terribly. I missed my family too, but I had so much more to lose than she did. I was still looking at thirty years in Angola, probably more now. Within one hour of learning about Candace's departure, fear turned to survival. I wondered if she had notified the US Marshal's Office about my location. Could she have betrayed me? No, from what I knew of her, I didn't think she could do that. But as much as I loved and trusted her, I wasn't going to take any chances. I quickly gathered together everything important to me and left, closing the apartment door behind me for the last time.

As I approached the entrance to this great forest... I took in one deep breath, exhaled and said, "Goodbye, world."

Chapter 6

Montreal, Canada and Gatineau Park – Alone

I knew a crook who drove cabs part time and he agreed to drive me from Toronto to Montreal. He didn't know I was wanted in Louisiana, but I told him I was wanted for auto theft in Toronto and needed to get out. For a fixed price, he dropped me off in Montreal. Montreal was a city even more beautiful than Toronto. The population spoke primarily both English and French, so in time I picked up some French fairly well. My first task, as usual, was to locate a chop shop. I set out to find the familiar, seedy characters lurking in the darker areas of the city. But for some reason, Montreal didn't have many crooks stealing cars and there was not a large market for automobile parts. Since my trade wasn't popular there, I had to think of some new way to make a dollar.

Initially, I stayed in a local mission for the homeless. Though far from glamorous, for a small amount of money it provided me with three meals a day, a bed, and I could keep up with the world's events by watching television in the downstairs day room. I met a few people in this shelter, but for a couple of days I met no one who knew how to hustle. Most of these homeless people were resigned to their status quo. They were content with a bed, three meals and being lazy. At night it was necessary to hide personal items such as cigarettes, candies or other small objects, because you could be sure that someone would steal them as you slept.

After a short spell in the mission, however, I was asked to

leave. My money had run out and I had no income to pay for my accommodation and meals. I was as broke as a busted pipe. I had to come up with some new way to survive. "What can I do now?" I wondered.

I went to the library and hung around there all day, browsing through the books while I racked my brain for ideas. It was then that I noticed a book on survival techniques. I pulled it down from the shelf and began to read. The book told you everything you needed to know in order to survive and live in the woods. I pored over its pages, absorbing the information, and began to wonder if this was my way out. "I wonder," I thought, "if this is my next challenge?" I pondered whether I would be capable of surviving long term in the woods, so as to simply "disappear" from society. Could I live off the land employing these survival techniques? The more I turned the idea over in my head, the more it seemed perfect. It would mean I had no accommodation costs, no utility bills, free food by way of the plants and whatever animals I could hunt, and best of all, no police. "I can do this," I decided. "I haven't failed any challenge so far."

So my preparation began. For the next thirty days, I read every book pertaining to wilderness survival I could get my hands on. I studied like a college student last-minute-cramming for an important exam, recording in my mind the likenesses of all manner of plants and fruits, both edible and poisonous. I read books on the living habits of forest animals and other books that taught me how to butcher them. I read manuals about weather, water purification, emergency first aid, fire-starting, tracking, trapping and how to set lures and nets. The last book I read was written by Thomas Bayes, an Englishman who devised what became known as Bayes' Theorem. Bayes wrote an important work on the laws of probability, chance, and the human reasoning associated with chance. This book was nothing to do with survival as such, but it provided me with a philosophy of life that became very useful to me for survival purposes.

All these subjects interested me much more than the techniques of law enforcement ever had and I felt a buzz of excitement and anticipation as I contemplated my new vocation. My aim was to evade capture for as long as I lived. I knew now with certainty, that if I became a skilled practitioner of wilderness survival, I could do it.

Between these intense reading sessions, I still needed somewhere to sleep at night. Eventually I hit upon the idea of going to hospitals. Every major hospital has a sitting-room for relatives of those in intensive care. The security in hospitals is not always all it should be, since the staff are always busy, and they have no real way of knowing whether or not you are there with someone. So I simply pretended that a relative of mine was in ICU. That section of the hospital didn't seem to be patrolled much by the security guards and no one ever bothered me.

For a few weeks leading up to my retreat into the woods I also attended a local day labor office to find some casual work. Many homeless people do this in the hope of making a little extra money. I took a few one-off, cash jobs to earn just what I needed to embark on this next phase of my journey. I had already written a detailed shopping list of everything I would need to survive.

* * *

After researching various Canadian forests, I had worked out the perfect location to live. When the time came for me to begin this next phase, I hitch-hiked the 100 or so miles from Montreal to Ottawa, the capital of Canada, and then made my way to what is now called Gatineau Park – a vast forest with almost 140 square miles of cover – located in Quebec's Outaouais region, just north of Ottawa. As I approached the entrance to this great forest, I looked back and took in one deep breath, exhaled and said, "Goodbye, world."

On the day I departed civilization as I had known it there were a few other people around, hiking through the woods, so I made absolutely sure that no one else saw me as I veered off the park trail and into the thickets. From there I walked deep into the woods and searched for a likely site for my camp. After a couple of hours I found what I thought was the perfect location. I prepared a clearing, unloaded my equipment and began arranging my new home. The trees towered around me and a gentle breeze accompanied the sounds of the forest. It felt like this was going to be a peaceful place to be. Throughout the evening I walked out from my new home in various directions and explored the immediate area, trying to familiarize myself with my new surroundings. I wanted to be fully aware of all available exit routes in the event that anyone stumbled across my camp.

As darkness fell that evening, I confess I was a little scared. Gatineau is an unbelievably beautiful forest, but I learned quickly that the trees, leaves, bushes and animals you see during the day take on a completely different dimension at night. Despite the fact that I had prepared meticulously and knew a great deal about this new environment, I was unprepared for the sinister appearance the forest takes on at night and, as the dusk turned to inky blackness, I seriously thought about packing my bags and getting out of there. The only thing that stopped me was one persistent and unanswerable question: *Where am I going to go if I leave?*

That first night I started a campfire at about 8 p.m. I did it to "test" my environment, rather than for warmth or to cook food. I built it some 300 feet away from my actual camp because I wanted to see whether it would attract the attention of anyone who might investigate who was out in the forest. I also wanted to test the maximum number of wood logs I could burn with the lowest amount of glow. I didn't want any unwelcome attention from forest rangers. My location was a tough one for anyone to reach, but I wasn't prepared to take any chances. I lit this same "test" fire every day for an entire week until I was sure that everything was fine.

My first night in the woods was terrible. I had purchased Vienna sausages and a supply of potted meat to last until I was able to develop and fine-tune my hunting skills. I ate some food and tried to get some sleep, but this proved very difficult. I managed short stints of sleep, but was constantly awakened by strange sounds. There was no moon, so I couldn't detect what was making the noises in the deep blackness. I finally woke up at around 7 a.m., cold and tired. My first task was to gather some wood and proceed to build a fire. In a short time the flames were crackling, I had a pot of coffee on the boil and I felt much better. The coffee was warming as I sipped it, but though the sun was beginning to break through the forest canopy, it was still downright freezing. It had never been this cold in Louisiana. Nevertheless, I felt that in time I would adapt to my environment. Before I entered the woods I had enjoyed all the conveniences of modern life. Now I knew I had to progressively wean myself off such conveniences and gradually integrate myself into rugged living.

I set out that morning on a long hike to further familiarize myself with the area. As I began to walk through the forest, the whole experience was breathtaking. It seemed to me as though I was the only human being in the world. As I walked, cold, crisp leaves crackled beneath my feet. I felt the brisk, fresh air gently flowing across my face. I observed leaves floating to the ground as if they were dancing. As I walked up and down gentle hills and deep ravines, I checked my compass and ground markers to make sure of my direction. I listened to the sounds of the forest, hoping that in time, all these sounds would make sense and become familiar. Occasionally, I heard a dead branch fall from a tree, quickly followed by what sounded like another branch falling in the distance – an echo, I presumed.

In the relative silence and peace of the daytime forest, I had a lot of opportunity to think. I thought a lot about New Orleans and the family I had left behind. I thought about Candace and wondered what she might be doing at that precise moment. The realization slowly dawned on me that if I succeeded in this venture, then I would probably die in these woods. So I figured I would never see her face again. I thought about my brothers and sisters and wondered how they were all doing. What did they think about my decision to flee? Were they sad, crying or disappointed? Were any of them searching for me?

I also thought a lot about Grandma and what she would make of my current circumstances. How sad she would have been, were she still alive. In her effort to admonish me to do the right thing, she would never have suggested that I run. But she was long gone now. I missed her every day, but I was glad that she didn't have to see my stupidity. She had often taken me to one side and told me, privately, that as the eldest she expected me to keep the family together. I had failed her in so many ways. I had hurt so many people besides myself. I had hurt my family badly.

I began to think back over my life, to times when I was in elementary school and the fun times I'd had with friends. I remembered all my teachers and all of my little girlfriends. It's strange what goes through your mind when you're alone and there is no one else to make conversation. I reflected on how I had run around the school playground, enjoyed playing basketball, and later lifted weights and read books. These and many other activities were fading memories now. Each of them somehow circled around to this one thought: *Of all the people in the world, how did I get caught up in a situation like this?* I brushed tears from my eyes as I thought of all my evil deeds and how they had brought me to this.

At times, I cried with so much sorrow and remorse that I could no longer see where I was going. At these moments I would sit down on some damp log and try to pull myself together. I wondered whether I could really see this trial through to the end and reasoned with myself that I could still give myself up, return home and face the consequences. Eventually, though, I dismissed such thoughts as weak. Difficult as this ordeal was, I valued my freedom too much to give in – if you could call this real freedom. Often, I wondered if I had committed myself to a more drastic type of incarceration than prison. I had willingly embraced banishment and isolation, left everything I had known to take up exile in this strange, lonely place. The forest, though it provided a haven from the authorities, couldn't speak to me, couldn't love me, couldn't ease my sorrow.

Occasionally I would look up into the sky to see an airplane cruising over. "I wonder if those people are going to Louisiana," I thought, "maybe even to New Orleans?" I adopted the view of a complete outsider to society, thinking how happy those people must be, visiting family and friends, flying off to exotic locations, laughing and talking, eating and drinking. When these thoughts persisted I put my head down and walked on… on and on through the woods, further and further. I tried to dismiss my feelings. "These thoughts, my memories, this loneliness – these are the only things that can hurt me now," I thought. "I have to be strong, determined, rise to this challenge."

I knew that I had to get to work and take a highly disciplined approach to life in the wilderness. "Every day that I survive in these woods," I told myself, "things will get better." I focused on the fact that every month that passed would minimize the pain, sorrow and remorse I felt. In the end the thoughts that taunted me and threatened my survival and endurance must subside. "If I can make it here for a whole year," I reasoned, "then I'll get over these emotions and everything will be fine." So, I walked and kept walking. I wanted to become knowledgeable about this forest, to know it inside out. I wanted to know if one leaf hit the ground or one branch fell, if one bird died or another was born. I had won every challenge in my life; I would win this one also.

* * *

I walked for hours on end that first day, trying to familiarize myself with the terrain. This forest was huge, stretching in every direction as far as the eye could see. "I could live here for the rest of my life," I thought, "and still not explore every inch of it." During my walkabout I saw dozens of lakes, numerous types of trees, hills, even small mountains. The forest was teeming with life and I saw animals of all shapes and sizes. At one point I was walking alongside a stream that flowed steadily down into a lake some distance away, and saw otters and beavers frolicking in the spray. Having all the time in the world, I sat down and watched them – it must have been for several hours. Being a city boy, I had only really seen such animals in the zoo in New Orleans. I was surprised by how much bigger these wilderness creatures seemed, compared to the ones in captivity.

As the day began to draw in and evening approached, I figured I ought to return to my camp, or "home", as I would come to refer to it in due course. As I neared the outskirts of my camp, I noticed a small bird lying on the ground near a tree, clearly in distress. It was chirping loudly; so loudly that if a passing carnivore heard it, it would make a nice, easy meal. After looking around I spotted the nest from which it had fallen and climbed the tree in order to place it safely back in its home. The nest contained its two siblings and, for a few minutes, I marveled at the sight before climbing down in case the mother returned.

As I arrived back at my camp, I felt proud of the fact that I had hiked several miles and successfully navigated my way back, equipped only with a compass and a basic topographical map of the forest. I had a set of homemade markers with which I could indicate key landmarks to aid my navigation and then a collection of other essential items. My kit also consisted of various knives, a machete, a .38-caliber pistol I had bought from a crook in Montreal, a box of bullets, gloves, a small pair of binoculars, a first-aid kit, water purification kits, a snake poison kit and other useful items for survival. To all intents and purposes I probably looked like a professional soldier. I meant to make this transition from city life to rural life as smooth and efficient as possible – even though it meant hiking with fifty or sixty pounds of gear.

I settled down in my camp and prepared dinner, working my way through my canned goods. "In a few more days," I decided, "I'll practice my hunting skills." Following a meal of potted meat, crackers and a little water, I sat under a nearby tree and just relaxed. I struggled not to think of life outside the forest, but I had resolved to avoid capture. As the sun began to set on my second day, I prepared myself mentally and physically for the night. I was still scared, as I wasn't accustomed to the outdoors. I worried about being attacked by bears or wolves. That night, though it sounded quite a distance away from my camp, I did in fact hear wolves and coyotes howling. All the information I had read told me that, naturally speaking, these animals would avoid contact with me. But when you are alone, outside in the pitch black, your mind convinces you otherwise.

I prepared for bed early that night, both scared and courageous at the same time. It's difficult to explain my feelings, but I was both afraid of the unknown and prepared for it. I lay down in my small tent, watching the flames of the fire I had lit dancing in the dark. I looked up at the night sky and the stars appeared to be very close. Small clouds passed across the sky, momentarily obscuring them, and the coyotes and wolves continued to communicate in the distance. Apart from them, the only sound that night was the wind rustling the leaves with an occasional gust. I held my pistol in one hand and a machete in the other, waiting for trouble.

I had positioned my tent with the entrance and rear between two trees. My campfire was positioned to the front and my camping gear was piled to the rear. I was surrounded and protected pretty well and felt able to handle any danger that might come my way. I was a light sleeper naturally, but just in case I installed a makeshift "alarm system". I had found and collected some old, glass soda bottles, discarded by past visitors to the forest. I strung them together and suspended them near to the perimeter of my camp. Should any animal or a person disturb the brush at the entrance of my camp, the soda bottles would make a clanging sound and give me early warning. Eventually, I fell asleep, but only for an hour or so at a time. Around three or four in the morning, I awoke suddenly when I thought I felt something touch my feet. I couldn't see or hear anything, but I was petrified, and after that I was unable to go back to sleep.

In the early morning hours of the third day, I prepared my coffee, which seemed delicious after my disturbed night's sleep, and sipped it under a cloudy sky. I curled up in a ball inside my tent, as snug as a newborn baby, and knew I had survived another night. As the cold, gray clouds passed overhead I thought about going hiking again. This time I would attempt to travel deeper into the forest. After finishing my coffee, I gathered my hiking gear and walked in a different direction to the previous day.

As I penetrated deeper into the woods, I saw an animal that I would hunt often in the coming months – white-tailed deer. This animal was relatively easy to hunt, kill, clean and eat. I watched as a herd grazed on snow-covered, hard-frozen grass. As I approached them, I noticed they were not too scared of humans. They were cautious, but didn't immediately run away. I saw various man-made hiking trails, crossing paths with the deer trails. I got up close to the deer trail and inspected it closely. I wanted to learn their unique smell and footprints. I observed what appeared to be a mink in the distance near a lake. I wanted to learn its footprints also. As I reached the lake, above me soared eagles and hawks in the sky searching for prey.

On this day, I witnessed much more than the previous day. I observed squirrels hopping from limb to limb, occasionally noticing my presence. The squirrels were not bright red or light brown as in Louisiana, but either jet black or a very deep brown. After a short time of walking out in the open I retreated back into the deep woods, afraid that I might be spotted by a passing ranger. I knew the forest was patrolled by a team of rangers, as I occasionally saw the tire tracks of off-road vehicles, but I wasn't sure whether they had any kind of night vision equipment or how much security they had in place in the areas I frequented.

I was still a little uptight and scared, but I noticed I had more resolve, a little more courage than the previous day. The rest of that afternoon, until the night, was uneventful, except for one thing. I had an urge to see those chicks again. I stopped by their tree and waited for the mother to leave. After she'd left I climbed up to the nest and carefully stroked the neck of each tiny chick. They had not grown a full coat of feathers yet. This family of chicks became my friends over the weeks. It was the only actual contact I had with anyone or anything.

Chapter 7

Life in the Forest

On the morning of my fourth day in the forest, as I exited my tent, I sensed a presence within my camp. Scanning around, I saw an animal looking directly at me, but as our eyes met it quickly turned and disappeared through the trees. I only caught the briefest glimpse of it and, heading over to roughly where it had stood, I could smell a scent I didn't recognize. A short distance away the shrubs and bushes rustled as though the animal was moving through them. I didn't pursue it, but looked at its tracks and examined them closely, eventually working out that it must have been a wolverine. I realized from its hasty exit that it wanted no part of me, but the experience left me a little shaken. This was the closest I had been to an animal weighing some fifty to eighty pounds – one that would fight ferociously if scared or provoked. It was a reminder that I needed to be alert at all times in the forest.

The next day when I was out hiking, exploring in a new direction, I accidentally stumbled across this wolverine's den. The wolverine is a stocky, muscular animal resembling a small bear, with large rows of sharp teeth. As I unwittingly disturbed this female in the process of nursing her cubs, she sprang at me, fortunately only sinking her teeth into the topside of one of my boots. I leaped in the air with fright, staggered backwards and managed to retrieve my pistol as the wolverine launched another attack. As it moved forward I fired and shot it in the side. It moaned, hissed loudly at me and sank to the ground. Soon after she died.

This was the first time I'd been attacked by a wild animal in the forest and my heart was pounding, my body shaking. After gaining my composure, I looked at the cubs who had been hissing and growling in their den. They approached their mother's dead body and laid their heads on her, whining. I wondered whether it would be kinder to shoot them as well, seeing as they were vulnerable to predators with no parent to protect them, but after a few minutes I decided I should let them live and let nature take its course. My body was still trembling as I hiked back to camp. "It was either me or the wolverine," I told myself. "What was I to do?" As I reached camp I paused some fifty feet away and made sure it was safe to enter. From that day on, any time I returned to camp I always made sure there were no intruders or wild animals about.

That evening, I reminisced about the family I'd left behind. I began struggling again with those sad memories, trying very hard to forget the past. I stretched down on the cold, hard ground and looked at the gray unforgiving clouds. As tears rolled down my face, I placed one of my gloved hands over my mouth, literally forcing myself not to cry. But this action only made things worse. I laid on the ground tossing and turning in emotional turmoil, trying to shake this sorrow off. Suddenly, I heard a large tree branch crack and thunder to the ground. The sound was so loud that I had my pistol in my hand again before I'd even thought about it. It scared me, but had the effect of snapping me back to reality. I stood up, weak, scared and in pain, but gathered enough strength to set about lighting a fire. "Robert," I repeated to myself, "you must win this challenge."

On the morning of the sixth day, I thought about those wolverine cubs back at the den. I hiked to the den and found them all still alive, curled up against one another, looking up at me as if they hated me. They were grieving, just as I was. Those cubs and I shared something in common. We had lost a loved one. Again, I considered erasing their pain with a shot to the head, but eventually left them alone. The least I could do was give them a chance to survive, just as I was surviving.

During the next couple of days, I revisited the wolverine nest frequently to see how the cubs were faring. I thought they might venture out into the woods and learn to hunt on their own. But one day when I arrived, I found them all dead. "That's what could happen to me," I thought, "if I become weak and vulnerable in this forest." I sat on the ground near the dead cubs and reflected on all I'd experienced thus far. I soberly realized this life would be filled with many unknowns. When I lived in New Orleans I never ran across wolverines, never saw a coyote, certainly never observed eagles flying above my head. This life would be difficult indeed.

In the days that followed I explored many points connecting north and east, south and west, with the help of my compass. I was quite proficient with this tool. It was one aid that gave me a degree of confidence in this vast expanse of land. Without it I would have only been able to travel very short distances from camp. I also began to practice and hone my trapping and hunting skills. The first animals I caught were small squirrels. I managed to clean and cook them pretty well. Next I caught a few birds with the help of a mesh net, but I couldn't enjoy eating birds, as there was so little meat on them. It never once occurred to me, however, to kill the small birds in the nest near my camp. They were my friends – more like family, in fact. I still had a supply of canned goods to fall back on, but my aim was to force myself to become a proficient hunter. I had to work up to killing a deer – a meat I was familiar with after enjoying this treat many times around Mardi Gras time in New Orleans. My pistol would serve this purpose well, but I was afraid some ranger might hear my gunshot. As I hiked, I would see white-tailed deer eating in the distance. I wanted to attempt to trap one, but they are extremely alert and can smell the scent of a human a mile off.

One day, as my supplies were running low, I decided I had to kill a deer. I climbed a fairly tall tree I knew, on the edge of a large clearing where I'd often noticed white-tailed deer grazing. As I sat on a large limb, I waited for what seemed like hours, but eventually I saw a deer on the other side of the clearing. It looked as though it sensed my presence, because it was constantly looking around. I knew that a pistol was not really the proper tool to kill a deer with – I would have had a much better chance with a rifle. I also owned a small bow-and-arrow set, but I wasn't comfortable using it yet. Still, I was confident I could hit a deer with a pistol, thanks to my police academy training. I was a skilled marksman. Nevertheless, trying to find a "kill spot" on a nervous deer from a distance with a small firearm was a daunting task.

I surmised that my best chance was to try and hit a major organ with a shot below and just behind the head. I had to wait another thirty to forty minutes before he was anywhere near me. Then I saw my best chance coming. Below me, about twenty-five to thirty feet away, another deer wandered very close to the large tree I was sitting on. He didn't see me and obviously didn't smell me because he paused to look at the other deer. I couldn't shoot him, because thick brush and other small trees partially shielded him from my sight, but the other deer approached this deer cautiously as if they knew one another.

As the first deer approached, I was perspiring and shaking profusely. I aimed my weapon, paused, used all the techniques my police instructors had taught me and fired. When I shot him, he jumped about three feet in the air, then ran under the tree I was sitting in and into the brush. The other deer ran like there was no tomorrow. I quickly scrambled down the tree to inspect my kill. I thought he must have fallen close to the tree. But he wasn't anywhere close. That injured deer traveled about 500 feet before he fell. When I finally tracked him down, via a trail of disturbed brush and drops of blood, I discovered him lying down, still alive. With my heart pounding I took out my machete, not wanting to waste a bullet, and killed him unglamorously with blood projecting everywhere. Afterwards I sat down, breathing heavily, and looked at him. He was a huge creature with deep-set brown eyes, large hoofs and the trademark white splash of tail. He was truly a majestic animal – but I was desperately hungry and had to survive.

Next came the moment of truth. I had never cleaned and gutted a deer before. The limit of my experience had been the odd raccoon or opossum in Louisiana. I convinced myself that cleaning a deer was no different. With my large, sharp knives I butchered the choice pieces of meat – the hind leg quarters, the front leg quarters, the chest area and also some ribs. I already knew that I had to clean and gut any animal well away from my camp, otherwise I would be sending an open invitation to the local bears and wolves to come and visit me. I managed to do this job reasonably successfully, but cooking the deer back at the camp was much more difficult. In the process of roasting the deer I probably burned and wasted half the meat. In time I would learn to refine my outdoor cooking practices and make the most of every kill.

This first kill of deer was very important to me. It was proof that I could survive, confirmation that another challenge had been overcome. As darkness came over the forest that night, I felt satisfied. I had hunted, tracked, killed and prepared a deer – a major achievement. I slept that night with a full stomach, content. I drifted off to the usual backdrop of coyotes barking and wolves howling and slept a little better than usual, though I was still on edge, sleeping lightly. Ultimately, I noticed I was jittery throughout my entire stay in the forest. I was never able to let my guard down.

The weeks turned into months and the months into a year. I didn't keep track of the exact number of days and months, but I knew I had been there for quite some time. As my hunting skills developed further I was able to catch all manner of animals to survive on. I ate deer, squirrels and other animals often and, when I was able, I enjoyed nothing better than the trout or perch you could catch from the lakes if you were patient. Often the perch came up close to the lake's edge, allowing you to spear them if you had a steady hand. The area was also full of ducks, so I had quite a variety of food on offer.

I had equipment (though sometimes antiquated) to deal effectively with every situation I might encounter. Tracking became second nature to me as well as navigating. Cleaning and gutting animals was no problem. In time I could almost spot an animal as well as they could spot me. I was a good survivalist – keen, sharp, deliberate and logical. After a while, I was so in tune with the life of the forest that I could recognize individual deer or squirrels. I noticed certain animals hung out in the same areas and I could tell if I'd seen the same animal before from their markings.

I only saw the wolf pack, who were so fond of singing me to sleep, on one occasion. Wolves are highly elusive creatures and this day I had traveled a long way from my camp. I was squatting on a ridge, high up on one of the taller mountains, looking down over the range when I spotted them socializing. It struck me how like people such a social group is. You can quickly spot the leader of the pack and the top female. The pack I saw included about five to seven wolves. They were licking one another and probably communicating with each other just like humans. I slowly slipped away and headed back to my camp. I had no wish to engage with these carnivores.

I was proficient in identifying all kinds of tracks except one. I would not see this particular type of track often, but when I did, it would stand out because it was unlike any other animal track. Typically these tracks would lead from the forest, along the path of the lake, and return to the forest. I thought it must be a mammal that possessed amphibian tendencies. Only now, years after leaving the forest, have I some idea what it was – probably a "fisher" cat – a small mammal something like a polecat. If this is what it was, I never saw one in the flesh. Occasionally I would see a bobcat, a large animal some two or three times the size of a Himalayan cat and quite ferocious – a predator I preferred to avoid. One time a bobcat saw me sitting in a tree. He watched at a standstill for five to six minutes before turning around and heading deep into the forest. I had a few trees that were favorite places for me to sit, for hours at a time, and observe other animals' behavior. I wanted to know what they ate, how they killed their prey, where they slept. I became an animal much like them.

* * *

I had some strange experiences in the forest, but none so strange as one time in the summer months when I was out hiking in the early evening. I was walking through a certain part of the forest when I glimpsed something running in the distance. I thought it must be some animal, though I couldn't make out what exactly. As I got closer, however, I was amazed to see that it was a naked man, running around laughing. Quietly I moved closer still until I could clearly see a group of around fifteen or twenty people, all stark naked, gathered around a small camp. Some people were cooking, some were eating, some were standing around talking, whilst others were running around – doing everything that tourists would do on a normal outing into the woods, just without any clothes on!

This freaked me out. I had never in my life witnessed such a thing. Bourbon Street or Royal Street in New Orleans, after 2 a.m., were known to contain some raunchy and exotic people, but never on a scale like this. This gathering, reminiscent of a Roman orgy, made the French Quarter parties look like church social events. I sat there, hidden in the forest, observing this for at least twenty to thirty minutes. Most of this time was spent trying to fathom out what on earth these people were doing. I thought it was some kind of outdoor party gone wild. But I saw naked people in this same area of the woods many times in the future and eventually concluded they must be some kind of secret nudist group. It was just a bizarre sight to see in the forest when you are used to seeing otters, deer and wolves!

For well over a year I was a woodsman, a survivalist, and a lone wolf in this forest. I lived there for almost two years with no human contact, conversation or social interaction, living off the land. As a result I talked to myself constantly out loud. There were times when I worried if someone could go insane like this, but I preferred to speak out loud rather than in my head. I remembered one of Grandma's favorite sayings: "It's alright to talk to yourself and ask questions – just don't answer back!" I continued hunting, trapping, eating game, viewing and observing, learning and living in the forest – all the while providing a running commentary for myself, as well as for the animals, the trees, and the moon.

Many nights I lay quietly, listening to the now familiar noises of the night, and thought about the adventures which lay ahead.

Chapter 8

Back to Civilization

Though right from the beginning I was pretty good at trapping and hunting, whenever one does something new or difficult for the first time, there is a certain degree of fear associated with it. One thing I found extremely helpful in the forest, if I found myself faced with an unusual or difficult challenge, was to break it down into component parts and deal with each one separately, rather than trying to tackle the whole thing in one go and becoming overwhelmed. My method was this: accept its existence, analyze it, learn from it, then master it. This approach came from Bayes' Theorem and I found it invaluable – perhaps the greatest single piece of information I took into the wilderness. It helped me to be methodical and logical about every component of survival.

After a while I exhausted all my modern conveniences and was forced to live strictly off what the land could provide. At this point, one has to think logically and clearly concerning all endeavors. Even though I had read voraciously and thoroughly all the material available to me on survival, the books couldn't reveal everything I might encounter. Survival books can tell you how to track such things as a rabbit, but they can't tell you where or when to set a trap. In many ways it was just the same as being trained as a police officer. They can teach you many things in the training academy, but not everything can be practically applied when you are facing a criminal on the street. Another reason why I had to act logically and carefully was to avoid injury. I knew that if I had an accident and broke an arm or a leg deep in the woods, it could prove disastrous. Of course,

I probably could have come out of the woods and got myself to a town for medical treatment, but I was a fugitive. I didn't have the luxury of solving such problems normally, so I went to great lengths to avoid them.

One challenge of the forest that I needed to conquer immediately was that of getting clean water for drinking. I knew where plenty of water could be found, but how could I purify it and make it drinkable? I couldn't risk drinking straight from the lake, so over time I refined a technique to produce clean water from scratch. I would dig a shallow hole in the ground, about eighteen inches deep, wide enough to hold a small receptacle I had brought along for this purpose. Then I would stretch a piece of plastic such as my waterproof poncho over the hole and receptacle. I made sure the hole was positioned where it would catch the sun's rays and then waited.

As the sun heated the plastic, condensation formed on the inside and dripped into my container. In time I learned to place a small rock in the center of the plastic to make it dip in the middle and guide the water in, not wasting a single drop. *Voila!* Instant water. It was a slow process, but I could manufacture one to two quarts in a couple of days. Three or four strategically placed holes provided me with a constant supply of water. This distilling process worked best in the summer months when it was hotter, which was when I needed the most water.

By using survival techniques such as these I was able to wean myself off every modern convenience. There were only two items I really missed and two problems I couldn't solve. The luxuries I missed were a candy bar which I loved called Chunky®, made from chocolate, raisins and peanuts, and freshly ground coffee. At home I used to drink coffee all the time. I just had to learn to live without it. The two problems I couldn't solve were the hair growth on my face and clipping my toenails. I owned two pairs of hiking boots that were my exact size, but my toenail growth eventually made walking a little uncomfortable. I wore holes in the five pairs of socks I had and, eventually, I had no socks at all. I solved the sock problem with a light cotton shirt that I ripped and wrapped around my feet, at least giving my feet some warmth and protection. I had taken few clothes with me, mostly five of everything I needed: five pairs of pants, five shirts and so on. Apart from that I had a lightweight jacket for the warm weather and a heavy-duty coat made specially for cold-weather survival. With my inability to shave, I must have looked like a wolf-man, but I wasn't concerned about my looks, only my survival.

I hadn't got the space to carry many luxury items with me into the forest, but to conquer boredom I did take three books with me. One was a book outlining Thomas Bayes' Theorem, the second was a book on plants and the third was a dictionary. The dictionary in particular became well worn, since I read it every night. Why a dictionary? I figured that a dictionary is a story in itself. I found it fascinating to read new words and understand their meaning and definition. As a result I built up quite a vocabulary! Apart from these little things, which helped to keep me sane, I found there was a lot to learn about the world around me. Self-reflection and total silence is knowledge in itself. Occasionally, I thought of my family and wondered how Candace was doing. I had nothing but time on my hands, so I thought of the many experiences and situations I had seen throughout my life. I still held to an atheistic view of the world, so I had no regrets. I simply concluded that life deals everyone a hand and you play that hand as best you can.

In time, I was so integrated into wilderness living that I forgot about most of the things we take for granted in everyday life. I forgot about the joy of driving a car, watching television. I even disassociated myself from all feelings to do with love. I loved no one and felt no love from anyone. Actually, this was a very tolerable situation for me. When you're alone, you simply think of yourself – there is no wife, no kids, no family to think of. I had very few needs, so I had very few problems. One of my biggest concerns in life was my toenail problem! "I wish I owned some nail clippers," I would tell myself frequently. Occasionally I would visit places in the forest where other campsites had been and would forage around, hoping to discover a discarded pair, but I had no luck. People often left all sorts of things behind, but never toenail clippers. "Boy, why doesn't someone lose a toenail clipper?" I thought.

To keep healthy, I exercised five days a week. I would do countless push-ups and at one time could do up to 500 without stopping. I would use thick tree branches to do pull-ups and then carry out a routine of sit-ups, squats and runs through the woods. I had taken ten bottles of multi-vitamins with me for the journey and they were like gold to me. I took one just once a week to help ward off any serious vitamin deficiencies.

After a long time in the forest I began to lose track of the months, becoming more attuned with the seasons, though I did manage to retain a rough sense of what day of the week it was. Often at weekends families would venture into the forest for recreation. I knew the landscape so well that I could immediately spot if a particular rock or track had been disturbed, and this would tell me it was the weekend. I would avoid moving about too much during the weekends, to avoid detection.

My scariest moment in the woods occurred one day while walking down a narrow trail. I surprised what appeared to be a bear with cubs just five feet off the trail. As soon as I saw it I turned and fled in the opposite direction. I had no wish to engage with an angry, defensive bear protecting her cubs! I don't think the bear gave chase, but I was taking no chances. One thing that my survival training had told me was that you never run from bears, but it's almost impossible not to run when one is standing right in front of you! The best and most peaceful times were late at night when I was lying on my sleeping bag, looking at the stars. It was incredibly serene. It often seemed strange to see so much beauty. The night sky was my sleep aid and I often fell asleep holding the scene in my mind.

* * *

After quite some time in my new home I started to develop my first physical problem. I awoke one day with blurred vision and everything seemed hazy. I panicked on that particular morning because I didn't know what was going on. It lasted all day and then came back intermittently for the next couple of weeks. After a couple of months of this, it suddenly got worse. I wasn't in any physical pain, but I couldn't work out what was happening or why. Whatever it was, though, it was getting worse and I knew it might only be a matter of time before my eyes quit working altogether. If that happened, I would be in very serious trouble. What if it was some sort of brain tumor? What if I simply didn't wake up one morning? The problem was getting so bad that I could no longer track animals properly. Eventually I would be unable to hunt and then I would not last long.

The problem was also having an effect on my mental stability and I suffered from a few panic attacks. Mental problems, just as much as physical ones, can be very serious when you are so far from civilization. Whatever this was, it was interfering with my ability to function, to survive. When one morning I woke up and could hardly see, except for objects very close to me, I knew I had to leave camp and get to the nearest city to investigate this oddity.

I was loath to leave the forest. This was going to be a serious challenge after spending so long utterly alone in the wild, living a lifestyle alien to most normal people. I had also developed an odd attachment to the young birds I'd befriended and had to convince myself they would be OK until I returned. Eventually, I headed out of the woods and toward the main highway which led southeast to Ottawa. As I walked I began to see cars, people, dogs, buildings and billboards – all for the first time in nearly two years. Exactly how long I had spent in the woods I didn't know.

* * *

A short while later I spotted a familiar vehicle in the distance heading toward me. It was the provincial police, a lone officer similar to a state trooper. I began to head off the road and toward a wooded area without making it look obvious that I didn't want to be seen, but he'd already noticed me and was pulling over. He lowered the window of his cruiser and asked if everything was OK. "Yes sir, I'm okay," I replied. He asked me all the usual cop questions: where I'd been, where I was going and so on. He didn't make any comment on my appearance, however, which must have been terrible. I decided to tell him the truth – that I lived off the land. He asked why and I told him it was due to my religious beliefs. I sold him a story that I was some kind of monk on a quest to find my inner self and made it sound as convincing as possible. He told me to get in the car and he would give me a lift into Ottawa. Reluctantly, I agreed and during the journey he bombarded me with all manner of questions, though none of them investigatory. He seemed to be simply curious about my living in the woods.

As we drove my eyes scanned the scenery all around, taking in the sights and sounds along the highway. For the first time in a couple of years I smelled the long-forgotten odor of my body, since this was the first time I'd been in a confined space, and I truly smelled terrible. The officer didn't comment, however. I was sitting in the rear of the vehicle, separated from him by the protective glass – fortunately for him! As he dropped me off he wished me luck. "If only you knew who I am," I thought to myself. If he had apprehended me, he would almost certainly have been promoted for arresting a high-profile fugitive. Normally a cop had to endure a battery of exams to climb the ladder, but catch a fugitive and *voila!* – instant upgrade! My departure from New Orleans had launched a frenzied hunt by the law enforcement agencies. I later heard that officers had laid bets on who would catch me first. My flight was the talk of the Department. Pity this guy didn't recognize me.

As I made my way into downtown Ottawa my senses were in overload as they were bombarded with the sights, sounds and smells of the city we all take for granted on a daily basis. My ears were simply not accustomed to such volume and diversity of sound any more. At one point I just halted on the sidewalk and stood there, trying to adjust to the bedlam going on all around me. Eventually, I adjusted enough to carry on and continued walking. Shortly afterwards I located the mission where I had stayed when I first came to Ottawa. The counselor on duty agreed I could stay there, but only if I took a shower, shaved and changed my clothes. He gave me some soap and shaving supplies and I proceeded to the showers. What a surprise! For the first time in many months I viewed my reflection in the mirror. No wonder the cop who picked me up hadn't batted an eyelid. I hardly recognized myself!

My plans in Ottawa were simple: find a doctor, find the problem, fix it and head back to the woods. I hated civilization. I hated people. In the woods I didn't have to deal with any of it. While I had been living my solitary life, my mentality had changed. I was more like an animal than a person. My sole purpose for living was hunting, stalking game, eating and sleeping. I wanted no part of society again. I had trained myself extremely well for this journey and I wasn't about to compromise that.

After cleaning myself up, I went to the accident and emergency ward of a nearby hospital and complained of serious head pains so that a doctor would see me immediately. After a thorough examination the root of my problem was identified and it was quite treatable: I needed glasses. The isolation of the wilderness had messed with my mind, causing me to think about brain tumors and the possibility of dying alone in the forest, but I only had an optical problem. I was very relieved to hear this and it meant my plans for heading back into the woods were on track.

However, I had one small problem. I had no money to go to an optician and buy glasses. What was I going to do? I resorted to what I knew. I still possessed car-stealing skills, so I figured it was time to resurrect my trade. All I needed was one car and one buyer. After searching around the seedy parts of town, I found a man who was interested in a certain kind of car. He said he had the ideal place for me to strip it, so we agreed on a price and I went to work. I searched and eventually located this car and very easily stole it.

While I was traveling to our pre-agreed rendezvous point, however, an Ottawa Municipal Police car turned onto the road right behind me. Initially I didn't panic. I had no reason to. But for some reason this cop decided he was going to pull me over. I guess the only reason for doing so was because I was a young guy driving a Jaguar.

In other words, I didn't fit the car. Sergeant Duke, back at the Police Academy in New Orleans, had taught us to always look for oddities in the process of detecting crime. Oddities such as young people driving expensive cars were definitely on the list.

The cop turned on his emergency lights to pull me over. I knew he would have already advised the radio dispatcher of his location and relayed details of the vehicle's license plates. Information about the vehicle being stolen would come back to him in a couple of minutes if it had been reported. I slowed down and came to a halt. He stopped behind me and got out of his car, but as soon as he neared my vehicle I floored the accelerator and fled. Running back to his cruiser, he got in and gave chase. I knew other police officers would join shortly as he called for back-up, so I had to lose him quickly. Eventually, I lost him by virtue of the speed-driving course I'd taken as a New Orleans police officer.

In my haste to get away and my desire not to be caught, I didn't have time to thoroughly wipe off every fingerprint as I abandoned the car. Panic flooded through me. I knew once a print was lifted, the local police would run it through the National Crime Information Center for identification and my name would show up. I did not know for sure if I'd left any usable prints, but I didn't want to take any chances. I immediately made my way to the nearest truck stop in a bid to get out of Ottawa. Fortunately, I met a trucker there almost straight away who was willing to give me a ride to Toronto.

Two hundred and fifty miles away in Toronto, I stopped to examine my situation. Earlier, when Candace and I had stayed in Toronto, I wasn't sure if she'd notified the US Marshals of our flight to Canada. Neither was I sure if I'd be identified from the stolen vehicle in Ottawa. I had to assume the worst. I presumed that the authorities knew I was in Canada, but just didn't know where. I decided now was the time to cross the border into the USA and go somewhere completely different. Back then, in the early 1980s, it was no problem for someone to cross the border between Canada and the USA, especially a pedestrian. The border patrol would probably think you were just going out for a day of shopping. I walked across the border and made it to Niagara Falls.

I had left all my camping gear in the forest and I needed to restock. While wandering around town that day I saw a small warehouse where many people were just standing around. My street smarts told me they were homeless people looking for work. As the foreman called for people who wanted to unload trucks, I obtained a spot. While unloading one of the trucks, I chatted with one of the truckers and learned he was going to Chicago via New York. I told him I was from Chicago and he agreed to give me a lift the next morning. I wanted to retreat to the woods again, but I figured it did not matter what state I was in. Almost all states have some sort of forest.

It sounds strange now, but the only thing that nagged me about moving on was my little birds near my forest camp. I guess they had become my surrogate family. In any case, they had probably left their nest by that stage and I needed to move on. I was headed toward Chicago.

Yet, he was by far (along with Grandma) the most honest, sincere, hopeful, and humble person I ever met.

Chapter 9

Chicago, Illinois – Father George Clements

I arrived in Chicago in the winter of (I think) 1982–83. I can only approximate the date, since I had lost all track of time while living in the wilderness. I would have been twenty-seven or twenty-eight years old.

During my frenzied escape from the Canadian authorities I had lost my coat, so I arrived in Chicago wearing a shirt, and it was freezing cold. Chicago was a vast, sprawling metropolis and this was my first visit. I wandered through the streets and tried to work out my next move. As the bitter winter wind bit at my body, I noticed a Catholic church called Holy Angels across the street. I was still very much a confirmed atheist. I hated anything to do with God. But, driven by my immediate practical need, I found myself crossing the road and heading toward the church. I felt sure that someone there would give me a coat if I asked. Many large, city center churches like Holy Angels kept a "pantry" for the homeless. I walked up to the church and knocked on the door.

Someone came to open it. It was a light-skinned black man with a receding hairline, wearing black priest's garments, who I guessed was in his fifties. He spoke to me, but so softly that I could hardly make out what he was saying. In due course I discovered he was the pastor of this church – Father George Clements. I didn't know it at the time, but Father Clements was something of a celebrity in Chicago. He was widely known throughout the city and was on a first-name basis with the current mayor of Chicago, Jane Byrne. I told him I was homeless and had no food or coat and asked him if he could help me. He casually questioned me about who I was, where I came from and so on, and I promptly gave him some answers to satisfy his curiosity.

During the conversation, Father Clements mentioned he needed to go and pick up his son soon. "His son?" I thought. "I've been in the woods a long time, but since when did Catholic priests start having children?" He must have spotted my expression because he then explained that it was his adopted child. Years later I discovered that Father Clements was the first ever Catholic priest to adopt a child, and it had received a lot of publicity in the media. He also founded an organization called One Church, One Child, the goal of which was to encourage every church in the world to adopt at least one child. He worked diligently in the community as a social activist.

Our introductions over, he led me to an upstairs bedroom in the rectory and told me to rest and get some sleep; he would attend to my needs in the morning. Grateful for this kindness and feeling that I could relax a little, I crashed into bed and slept for a long time. I was awakened the next morning by the sound of several people talking outside my door. Cautiously, I peered outside to see what was going on. In the next room Father Clements' office was a hive of activity. All sorts of people were coming in and out with various needs; staff were typing letters and directing many different aspects of his ministry's affairs; other priests were conversing with parishioners; all manner of business was going on. It was obvious that Father Clements was much in demand.

I retreated into my room and lay on the bed, listening to the buzz outside for about an hour, and then decided to see if I could get to speak to him. I walked into the office and saw Father Clements speaking to some lady. He was helping her with her utility bills. I caught his eye and he motioned for me to step into his office. Once inside I was struck by the fact that everything in his office was either black or white, and I mean everything: ceiling, rugs, ink pens, pictures, papers, everything. I passed comment on the color scheme, or lack of it, and he told me that it represented white and black people standing together. Then he spoke about his hopes for peace in the world and how much he loved people. He was a softly spoken and clearly highly intelligent man.

He then directed his attention toward me and asked me a question. It was nothing to do with my needs; he wanted to know if I played chess! I told him I knew how to play, but didn't often get the chance, so he immediately invited me to have a game with him. He beat me soundly and quickly. Much later I learned that he was a world-class player who had hardly ever been beaten. No wonder he dispatched me in record time! After we finished playing he looked at me across the board and said, "Robert, chess is very similar to the game of life. All outcomes in life are based on the decisions we make. The key to winning at chess is preparation, a plan of action, and then the tenacity to carry out that action."

After that I listened quietly as he told me more about his travels across the country to encourage people to love one another and to eradicate racism. He spoke at length about the world's problems and I couldn't help thinking to myself, "Please just shut up and give me a coat!" He was obviously a nice man with a good heart, but I couldn't tolerate all this crap about God and his love. My only concern was getting a decent coat. It was about ten degrees in Chicago and I only had a shirt on. I didn't even particularly want to sleep in the church – the walls of my room were covered with the kind of religious trash that Candace had been fond of, that had annoyed me so much back at our apartment in Toronto.

Finally, Father Clements finished his sermon on love and said to me, "Let's take a ride." We jumped in his car and he took me into downtown Chicago – a big, buzzing, beautiful city. As we walked the streets, all kinds of people walked up to him and shook his hand. Within a two-block radius at least fifteen people greeted him. Eventually we entered a fancy department store. Father Clements told a store clerk to fit me for a coat. In due course he purchased the most expensive coat I'd ever owned, costing around $200.

Afterwards, we went across town to visit the Cardinal's

residence. This man was the head of Chicago's Catholic churches and highly revered. Father Clements introduced me to the Cardinal and then the two of them left me alone while they chatted about church affairs in the next room. While I waited, I wandered around the large, opulently furnished house reading all sorts of plaques and honors that had been bestowed upon the Cardinal.

As we drove back to the rectory, Father Clements asked me where I was staying. I told him I was homeless and he said he knew several people who could give me a job. I decided to take him up on this very gracious offer. As we continued driving I also asked him if he knew of an optometrist. He said one of his best friends was an optometrist! So he drove directly to the doctor's office. When we arrived the doctor was examining a patient, but he stopped in the middle of the examination to greet Father Clements. In less than one hour I was fitted with a pair of glasses at no charge. I began to realize what an amazingly well-connected man he was.

Later, we arrived at an apartment in an upscale part of town. He said this apartment was owned by the church. Priests visiting from out of town would stay there instead of a hotel. He told me I could reside there temporarily until he and I could plan what I would do with my life. Even though he had only just met me, Father Clements had given me a job, better eyesight, clothing and an apartment.

The next day, Father Clements picked me up from the apartment and we drove back to the office at Holy Angels Church. He introduced me to his son, Joey, who was around seventeen. Joey lived in the church rectory where he had his own room. Father Clements said he had an appointment to attend to and left me and Joey to get acquainted. Though I was around ten years older than Joey, we hit it off right away. We talked about what he knew of his past before being adopted by Father Clements. Joey was a jovial character – the type of person who is always laughing and smiling – and I enjoyed talking to him immensely. Of course, I could tell him very few details about my real life, so I kept the conversation very general. We played a few games to keep ourselves amused and had a pleasant afternoon. Later, when Father Clements returned, we all went out and ate at a local Chinese restaurant that he liked. All of us especially enjoyed the egg *foo yung* that night, and this set a trend. In the weeks and months ahead the three of us would get together and eat egg *foo yung* often.

Father Clements had promised to get me a job and he was true to his word, but I ended up working for him! I vacated the church's apartment, which was really meant to entertain visiting speakers, and lived in the rectory for several months. During that time Father Clements invited me to accompany him on various social functions and church events. As we talked and I came to trust him more, I told him a little about my former life, revealing that I had once been a police officer. Part of my training, I told him, had included specialized security procedures. At this point he decided that I should become his "personal assistant" (or, more appropriately, his bodyguard, since people mobbed him wherever he went) and he would pay me out of his own salary.

After I'd been in Chicago for a year, Father Clements and I were firm friends. He was a champion of those in need and continually upheld the cause of the downtrodden. There were a great many homeless people on the streets of Chicago and frequently, as we drove around the city, he would pull over and stop to help someone. No one can spend a lot of time around someone like that and not be affected by them; his thoughtful, caring attitude was contagious and it began to rub off on me. If I saw someone in need as we were driving, I suggested we stop and help them. If I was watching the news and saw that some poor person's home had burned down, I would mention it to Father Clements and we would visit and try to assist this person. Numerous times some destitute person knocked on the church office door looking for help and I gave them money.

Around this time I met a wonderful lady called Mary and we formed a close relationship, eventually living together, sharing an apartment. Mary was a carbon copy of her mother and one of the kindest and gentlest women I had ever met. She was such a kind person that I thought to myself, often, how undeserving I was to come across such a lady. To protect her anonymity, I won't write much about her here, but two children would come out of this relationship

– a girl and a boy, born close together. I loved being a father and for a while, everything seemed idyllic. Little did I know then, that just like my father, I would end up having nothing to do with those kids' lives. This life I had chosen would take me on many twists and turns and leave many casualties in its wake. I would badly hurt these children, and not just them, but other children too.

* * *

After about eighteen months I became something of a personal executive assistant to Father Clements. Gradually I handled more and more of his personal business affairs and he trusted and confided in me. I looked after his itinerary, since he was invited as a guest to nearly every major gala or social gathering in Chicago. But I knew his heart was to spend time with ordinary people, so many smaller local charities and social organizations received the privilege of having Father Clements speak at their functions at my request. If he had a full appointment schedule, I was the only person who could alter it. After two years had gone by, I knew I was considered a fully fledged member of the Clements family. During the time we spent together, I think I was the only person who ever referred to him simply as "George". We played chess almost every day and he won every game.

For a long time I wondered to myself if Father Clements was for real. Some might find it strange that I should question his integrity, but remember, all my life, apart from my Grandma, most of the people I'd known were crooks, liars, thieves and fakes. Here was a man who, along with Grandma, was the most honest, sincere, humble and hope-filled person I had ever met. It was hard to reconcile with my own flawed character.

Even if Father Clements got annoyed or became angry about something, he did so in a measured, controlled way, never totally losing it or yelling at anyone. I remember one occasion when I upset him. I asked him to come with me to visit a lady who was destitute and sleeping in a mission. He was extremely tired that day, having already had a very full week of events, speaking engagements, and visits to his parishioners. I should have known he was just plain tired, but I persisted. He gave in and we went to help the lady. As we were driving back to the church office, however, he didn't speak a word. In time, as I learned his temperament, I noticed that he dealt with anger through silence. This actually became a great example for me to follow; it helped me to consciously and deliberately deal with my own anger. I realized that I could discipline myself mentally and become a more patient person. Father Clements was the only person I knew who really resembled Jesus and sought to practice his teaching in his everyday life.

One day I left my apartment, not far from the rectory, to see Father Clements. As I walked into his office, I was amazed to see US Representative Harold Washington of Illinois. Also in Father Clements' office were some other big-name contributors to his ministry and local councilmen from various Chicago neighborhoods. I had walked in on something of a secret political meeting. They were discussing Representative Washington's political run for the mayorship of Chicago. Eventually, Harold Washington would indeed become the first and only black mayor in Chicago's history.

Some of the strategies for his election were hammered out in Holy Angels Church, in Father Clements' office. From then on, I saw Mayor Washington almost weekly, as well as other celebrities such as Jesse Jackson, former Mayor Jane Byrne, a very young teenager named Janet Jackson, Zev Braun who was a movie producer, and many others. I said Father Clements was like a celebrity! Eventually someone turned his life story into a major motion picture.

After about two years of living in Chicago, although I had a good job, a great relationship and a roof over my head, problems began to surface in my character and I got into a bad habit. It seemed as though whenever I had a chance of being happy and settled, something in me would derail that happiness and it would all go down the drain. Even when I was staying still in one place, I was running on the inside.

I had started going regularly to the horse track with a janitor from the rectory. What started innocently as a recreational pastime had soon developed into something much more serious. I was gambling heavily and uncontrollably. I had become addicted to the buzz of it. So much so that I was about to do something very wrong and stupid.

During the entire time I stayed with Father Clements, I never took a dime from him. There was no need to. But I needed money and one day I noticed that he had a safe in his private quarters. In it was kept all of the Sunday mass donations. I had no idea how much money would be in there, but it turned out to be around $2,000 in cash. I sneaked into his bedroom to look over the safe. It's not easy to crack a safe, but I was a good crook and had never backed down from a challenge. I began to reason with myself and excuse the crime I was about to commit. I convinced myself that I wasn't going to take all the money – I just needed some of it to tide me over.

It took me around two weeks to figure out how to open the safe, but eventually I did it. I won't divulge the method I used. I stole around $200 every other day to fund my gambling enterprise. All the time I was breaking and abusing his trust like this, Father Clements and I would continue to sit and play chess every day. My deceit knew no bounds. One day, I opened the safe and found there was no cash in it. He had deposited it at the bank. Only his personal checks remained in the safe. So I took a blank check from the pad, filled it and cashed it for $200. As always, whenever I did something wrong in life, I regretted it not even one hour after I'd done it. Stealing from Father Clements was no exception.

He knew full well that I was no saint. For a start, he realized that I did not acknowledge God in any way. He probably suspected that I was an atheist, though he never asked me directly, and I had frequent, heated debates with him and the other priests about God. But he still treated me like a son and certainly did not deserve my evil deeds. When he eventually discovered my betrayal, he was hurt, shocked and disgusted. He approached me and we talked about what I'd done. I knew there was no point in trying to hide it. Trust is a very difficult thing to repair; in some cases, it's impossible to get it back. He told me that of all people, I was the one person that he'd truly trusted. He gave me thirty days to leave the apartment. He said I could still come and visit him, but I could no longer live there, and he instantly took back all the keys to the various church doors.

It tells you something about the kind of man Father Clements was that he didn't throw me out immediately and have nothing more to do with me. The fact that he gave me thirty days to put my affairs in order was miraculous. What was even more miraculous was the fact that, though he was upset with me for about a week following this incident, he still asked me to play chess with him every day. When the day came for me to move out, I went to the rectory to return the apartment keys to him. He was hurt to hear me say I was leaving Chicago. He told me he forgave me for what I'd done and wanted me to stay. It was a great offer, but I had realized something: I missed the solitude of living in the woods. I had been living a "normal" life for two years now, but I had not made a success of it. Try as I might to acclimate myself to my domestic situation, I couldn't do it. Relationships always seemed difficult. I was better off on my own, I thought. We played one last game of chess before I left. I whipped him so badly he had to loosen his white priestly collar. He was shocked. He then asked me what scheme I devised to finally beat him. "The same scheme I used to get into that safe," I replied.

Chapter 10

Memphis, Tennessee – an Encounter with Law Enforcement

hough I had initially planned to return to the wilderness and resume my former outdoor life, instead I headed for Memphis, Tennessee. Why Memphis? A few months earlier I had accompanied Father Clements there on a business trip, and while he attended his meetings I explored the city. While I was walking outside the Peabody Hotel, a hustler approached me and asked if I wanted to buy some gold jewelry. I wasn't interested in his gold, but while we talked I asked him if he knew of any chop shops in town. My mind was never far from crime. He told me about a guy named Bubba who lived not far from where we were standing. He even offered to take me there, but since I was new in town I wouldn't just take off with some stranger. I did remember this name, however, and mentally filed it away. If I ever returned to Memphis, I thought, I could resume my car-stealing enterprise.

After leaving Chicago I felt drawn back there – a new city, a new state. I was always on the move. If I got too comfortable somewhere, that's when I was in danger of being caught. When I arrived in Memphis I had enough money to rent a hotel room not far from the mid-city area. I checked in and immediately looked up Bubba to see what he was in the market for. It took me all of five minutes to locate him. He was a little uneasy about speaking to a complete stranger, but I persuaded him that I was a crook, just like him.

On my way back, I stopped at a little neighborhood store to buy a cigar. I struck up a casual conversation with the owner about which brand of cigars we preferred and then left the store to walk the remaining six blocks to my hotel. I was less than a block away from my destination when five Memphis Police cars came out of nowhere, each from a different direction, and cornered me. They took me so much by surprise that I had no time to react. The officers scrambled out of their vehicles, weapons drawn, and yelled for me to hit the ground. I couldn't believe what was happening. "After all this time," I thought, "this is it. They've finally caught me."

I managed to ascertain, however, by staying calm and speaking to one of the officers, that they weren't apprehending me as a fugitive from justice. The store I had just left had been robbed just minutes after I'd walked out. The store owner had called the cops and given them a description. Unfortunately, the real culprit looked similar to me and they had arrested me because I fitted the description. As they were preparing to take me in, I spoke quietly to one of the officers. I told him I hadn't robbed anyone and pleaded with him to convince his colleagues to take me to the store owner. "He'll tell you it wasn't me who robbed him," I said. The officer pondered this and went to discuss it with the others. I knew that if they took me in, that would be it. As soon as they fingerprinted me they would know that I was wanted in Louisiana.

The cops finally agreed to my request, but said they wanted to speak with the victim first. We returned to the store and as we arrived, the owner came outside, visibly shaken by the trauma. He looked at me and told the officers they had made a mistake – I wasn't the guy they were looking for. They released me on the spot. I felt huge relief as I walked back to my hotel. "If only they knew who I was," I thought. But despite this close call, the next night I stole a car, stripped it and sold the parts and got myself an apartment.

Within a few months of being in Memphis, I met a nice young lady named Veronica who was much younger than me. Once again I began a new relationship in a new town, giving away very little information about my past life. Within a short while she became pregnant and nine months later my third child on the road, a girl, was born. Sadly, I was not destined to play any part in her life in the future.

Our apartment was quiet, the perfect place for a fugitive. There was no onsite manager, no lease and no peeping old ladies. My next-door neighbor was a man called Thomas, who was the pastor of a local Baptist church. He was living there temporarily while his home was being remodeled. Each evening I would sit on the steps outside my apartment and Thomas came out regularly to proselytize me and talk about God. I told him I didn't believe in God, of course, but this didn't deter him and he persisted in trying to convince me that God was there and that God loved me. We had numerous heated debates and he began to try my patience. I knew I needed to move away from him, fast. He was tenacious with all this God crap.

One day, as I sat in the rear of my apartment to escape Reverend Thomas' debates, he came looking for me. Though I wasn't in the mood to hear his sermon, he told me he had just returned from officiating at a funeral at his church and explained how he knew this deceased person was now in heaven with Jesus. I asked him how he knew that exactly. In response he went on and on about believing in God and what God said in the Bible and so on.

I waited until he'd finished preaching at me and then asked him, "If I told you I was going to the supermarket, but did not go, how would you know where I was? And if you don't know where I'm going on this earth, how can you speak of heavenly journeys which you can't see?"

He attempted to counter my logic, but every theory he came up with, I shot down with more analogies, theories and concepts designed to disprove his points.

After thirty minutes of this duel he stood up and said, "You are one ignorant, stupid person." Then, he used a curse word.

I laughed at him and asked, "Where's your faith? Where's your patience? Speak up, Thomas!"

As he walked away, he muttered that his name was Reverend

Thomas, not Thomas.

I shouted back, "What's on your birth certificate?"

With that he turned around and approached me again, cursing in my face.

I stared him straight in the eyes and told him, "This is the problem with you so-called preachers today. You talk all this crap about God, but you find it difficult to manifest his teachings."

As I continued, he stood there looking at me sternly, obviously furious.

"Animals are more reliable in life than you people are," I carried on. "You read, but you don't comprehend. You preach, but you don't follow. You constantly tell people what to do, but you don't do it yourself. You are a hypocrite, a fool and a liar."

By this time his wife had come outside to see what all the commotion was about. I carried on as if she wasn't there. "You are here on earth speaking about heavenly and metaphysical subjects, but you can't master terrestrial subjects," I declared. "Tell me, if God made Satan and Satan is evil, why did God make him? And if evil is such a bad thing and God made it, does not God approve of his creation? The first lie was from the beginning of the Bible, in Genesis 1:1."

Then I dared him to explain how his God made the sun on the fourth day *after* he made the trees, which happened on the third day. I asked him to explain how this was possible, since it is a scientific fact that you need the sun to grow a tree through a process known as photosynthesis. Finally, I said, "And while we're on the subject of Genesis, what is this light God speaks of on the first day if it's not the sun?"

At this point, a couple of our neighbors came outside to see what was going on. Undeterred, I continued to challenge Thomas, dissecting Genesis and preaching my own anti-God sermon. I ranted for a good thirty minutes, hardly taking a breath, while Thomas and his wife stood there staring at me, not saying a word. When I'd finally done, I went back inside my apartment, leaving the neighbors to whisper among themselves.

A couple of hours later, as I left my apartment to go out, Thomas was sitting in a chair outside. As I passed him I noticed he was studying his Bible – the book of Genesis. I smiled inwardly. "You're the ignorant stupid fool," I thought to myself. After that day, Thomas never spoke to me again. As a matter of fact, none of my neighbors spoke to me again, not even to greet me. This was OK with me. As far as I was concerned, I was at peace again.

I continued to steal and sell car parts until things got hot for me in Memphis. Apparently, Bubba the chop shop owner got busted with stolen goods in his house. I knew it was just a matter of time before Bubba ratted me out, and that meant only one thing: another broken relationship, another child abandoned, more broken hearts. But I had to put it behind me. I got on the next bus heading out of Memphis and didn't look back.

If you tied and bound me with a piece of rope, I could not escape simply by believing I'd be free. I could not be freed through faith...

Chapter 11

Asheville, North Carolina; Nashville, Tennessee and the West – Friendship

From Memphis, I traveled some 500 miles, eventually arriving in Asheville, North Carolina. It was 1987–88. Asheville was a small, quiet town and very beautiful, not far from the Great Smoky Mountains, and immediately I realized how much I had missed living in the woods after two years in the bustling conurbation of Chicago. I had enough money to purchase new camping gear, so I assembled all the tools and supplies I would need and headed toward the mountains to search for my new home. Though I had reintegrated myself into "normal" society – in practical terms at least, if not in my mind – as soon as I stepped into those beautiful woods, my survival instincts flooded back and took over once more.

In terms of climate, the Great Smoky Mountains were a much easier environment to live in. The winters there were far less harsh than the bitter Canadian winters. The only drawback was the increased presence of park rangers. The rangers tended to be much more vigilant inside a national park and I needed to work hard to avoid them. Nevertheless, I quickly found a location that would be hard for the rangers to find or to reach. Just as before, after a few weeks my supplies of canned goods ran out and I began to hunt and eat small game. This time, I was smart enough to purchase some toenail clippers.

I lived in the Smoky Mountains for one to two years, once again losing track of precise times and dates. I enjoyed my time in this beautiful place. But once again, circumstances would conspire to move me on. One day, while I was out hunting game, unfortunately I followed a set of tracks that led me right across the path of a park ranger. He stopped and got out of his vehicle to question me, asking me whether I was a day visitor or if I had a campsite. I lied, telling him that I was a day visitor, but I knew he suspected I was lying. After we parted company, he watched me closely as I entered the woods. Once out of sight, I circled back and took up a vantage point where he would not spot me. A little while later, I saw him go back to the point at which I'd entered the woods and begin looking around. He was definitely spying on me.

A short time later, another ranger in a truck pulled up and they both began searching the woods. I knew I was hot from that moment and, sadly, it meant I had to leave the mountains quickly. If the rangers caught me and then involved the local police, I would be in obvious trouble. I had already located several shortcuts leading out of the forest to use in such a situation as this, so I simply abandoned all my camping equipment once again and took flight.

I hated leaving. It had been a great place to live.

After making my way back down to Asheville, I hitch-hiked back to Tennessee, though this time to Nashville. The local missions were always a quick and easy resource to use in order to get some food and shelter, so I found one downtown and stayed there while I calculated my next move. While eating at the mission one evening I got talking to a guy named Lee. Our conversation was general and vague, with both of us circling around issues, so I knew instinctively that Lee was running from something, just like me. He told me he was planning to leave Nashville and head to the west coast. He also happened to mention that whenever he traveled he took the train. I was curious, since I had always moved around by catching buses or hitch-hiking. Lee insisted it was a better way to travel.

Lee and I got along really well. From our conversations I learned that he was a very methodical person, like me. We liked each other so much that we decided to travel together. Lee knew all the train routes inside out and taught me all the tricks he employed for hopping trains free of charge. I quickly learned that even if you're not sure where a train is headed, its cargo can tell you a great deal about where it is going and where it has come from.

After a couple of days of getting to know Lee, and with nothing to keep me in Nashville, I decided to head west with him. We went down to the Nashville rail yards and sneaked in. Here Lee coached me on how to jump on a moving train. Then he quickly identified a train that was headed west out of the yard and we prepared to jump it. As it rumbled past, slowly gathering momentum, Lee jumped aboard. Then it was my turn. I tried to jump on, but was unsuccessful. I tried a second time, but failed again. By now the train was picking up speed. I tried a third and final time, but didn't make it. It was going to take me a while to figure out this technique! Rather than abandon me, Lee jumped off the train. The car he had managed to get on was about half a mile down the track by now, and as he walked back to me I could see he was angry. He told me we would have to wait a couple more days to catch another train and said he should have stayed on it. We argued a little more about the train and Lee finally said to forget about it.

Later I thought about what a good friend Lee was becoming. He could easily have left me behind, taken off on that train and never given me another thought. The fact that he came back for me said something. He said he enjoyed hanging out with me, as I did with him. For the next three days we sneaked back into the train yard and Lee made me practice my technique on trains that were parked in the yard. Finally, when the time came to catch the actual train out of the yard, I jumped it with no problem – another challenge conquered. We headed out west, hopping on and off all types of trains along the way.

Lee was around six feet tall, white and slim, weighing around 150 pounds. He was a softly spoken, reflective type of person who never displayed any meanness or aggressive behavior. I deduced through our many conversations that he had become more spiritually minded or religious after he'd fled from whatever trouble he was in. He hadn't told me at first that he was wanted; I'd just assumed he was, because he exhibited all the telltale signs. Later he admitted it to me. Being a quiet, reserved person, Lee didn't really know how to handle himself and I couldn't imagine him faring very well if he ever got into a fight. Sometimes as we rode the trains, other hobos we met purposely spoke down to Lee, but he never rose to it. He didn't seem to have any backbone. The only "fight" Lee ever rose to was when we fought over our view of God.

On one occasion we ran into a couple of dubious-looking guys who knew Lee from a few years previously. One of them began aggressively questioning Lee about a bag he had loaned him, saying he wanted it back. I didn't know exactly what this was about, but Lee looked terrified, so I quickly stepped in and told the guy to back off and leave us alone. The man looked me up and down and, after a brief scan, figured I could handle myself. I was never scared of anyone and I guess it showed. The two of them retreated and didn't bother us again. Later, I learned that Lee was known as a pushover or wimp in the fugitive subculture. But word got out fast about this guy who now traveled with Lee.

One night Lee and I went to hop on a particular train, but in the process we discovered that behind every sliding door the compartments were full of products. Because we couldn't get in, we were forced to ride the train outside on one of the steel platforms that linked the rail cars. It was a cold, dark, moonless night and we sat huddled together in a tight space, shivering from the chilling air. But we couldn't see where we were going and when the train followed a sudden curve in the tracks, we were both flung off and went tumbling down a grass bank and over the edge of a deep ravine. After we had gotten over the shock of this and dusted ourselves off, we realized we were lucky to be alive. We had sustained some minor cuts and bruises, but were generally OK. We laughed at the fact we'd survived this ordeal intact. There was no way to catch up with the train, so after climbing out of the ravine, we walked for many miles, trying to orient ourselves again, since we didn't have a clue where we were.

As we traveled we stayed in numerous cities such as Little Rock, Oklahoma City, Lubbock, Santa Fe, Albuquerque and finally Salt Lake City. We used my survival skills to camp and live in the woods along the way, and Lee's transportation skills when we wanted to travel. I would hunt and catch food for us, but generally Lee did not care for wild game, preferring to go and eat in town at one of the local missions. It was one day at our campsite in Salt Lake City that Lee confessed to me he was a fugitive. He was wanted for attempted murder in New York City. He was very candid about everything, so I told him all about my flight from New Orleans and was quite candid also. Lee never believed the part about me having been a police officer, though. Every time I told him about something I'd learned on the force, he just laughed.

On another occasion, Lee and I were in the woods in New Mexico. We'd been forced to camp a long way from civilization this time, so Lee couldn't walk into town to get food. I trapped some small wild game for us, cleaned and gutted it and then began to cook it. As I was cooking, I noticed Lee staring at me. I was just about to ask him what was wrong when he stated in a serious tone, "You are really into this, aren't you?"

"Into what?" I asked.

"All this camping, hunting and running."

"In the beginning," I told him emphatically, "I knew *nothing* about surviving. It's just become a necessity in my life."

"But you act as if you're a chef in a restaurant," he fired back, "butchering and cooking animals like that. And when you go to sleep it's as if you're settling down in some fancy hotel for the night!"

I explained to him that I had simply accepted my plight and, through acceptance, I had learned to be efficient. But as we talked further, I realized that he despised the ease with which I lived, while he felt terrible about his own situation. He told me he thought I was "too happy" about my circumstances and added that we were both sinners and should be repenting. I told him that it was easy to make assumptions about me, based on face value, but that the man he observed before him had been cut down, torn asunder and toughened – a process resulting in the person he knew today. Furthermore, I explained to Lee that he was not privy to my earlier life as a fugitive. He had not seen the tears and sorrow I experienced in Canada. He had never witnessed my family's sorrow and pain. He did not feel the degrading embarrassment that Candace and I suffered in our neighborhood or hear the whispers as we shopped in the local stores. He did not experience the terror I felt while in jail, or the terror I endured in the woods of Canada.

None of this seemed to wash with Lee.

"But I have never seen you get on your knees and thank the Lord for anything," he fired back again. "I have not seen any contrition or remorse in you, Robert. It almost appears as if you prefer this life, as opposed to a normal life."

I continued to chew and enjoy my wild game.

"Lee," I said eventually, "I have come to accept this life as normal. I have perfected loneliness to an art and silence to a science. I cannot have a 'normal' life, as you call it. But it doesn't matter. I don't have any aspirations, causes or struggles. Through this struggle, I am an entity and a law unto myself. I serve no one but Robert. To me, the sweet roasted smell of deer or rabbit are the same in my stomach. That person in Louisiana died, but I am alive now! I will survive by whatever means I deem appropriate."

"You have become one with Satan," Lee said, with great sadness on his face.

After this intense conversation, I laid on my sleeping bag and prepared to go to sleep. With my eyes half open, I observed Lee walk over to my skillet of wild game simmering over the fire. He reached and helped himself to a piece of meat – the same meat just cooked by Satan. Lee and I were buddies and I loved him like a brother. "We just have to agree to disagree on issues such as this," I thought.

Even though he was wanted for a serious crime, Lee was very spiritually aware. He believed in God and he frequently prayed that somehow his nightmare might end. As we traveled through various towns, I thought nothing of stealing anything and everything I needed to survive, but Lee never stole anything. He had been on the run for approximately five years when I met him. He told me often how much he regretted what he'd done back in New York City.

One time, we had a bad argument. He knew I did not speak of God very much, but he did not know I was a militant atheist. When I finally told him, we began to argue constantly about God. Here we were, two fugitives from the law, sitting in the middle of the woods arguing about God! I always found it slightly surreal and ridiculous. But Lee believed God was going to provide a way for him to return home. I simply believed God had nothing to do with such things. As far as I was concerned, man dictated his own destiny through logic, preparation and choice. I often thought that Lee would get caught soon because he simply had too many ethical and moral issues about running, which meant he had already compromised his position.

At one point, as we argued about God's existence, I got in his face and yelled, "If God exists and he has power, then why don't you give yourself up and depend on God?" Lee didn't say anything, he just stared at me. That evening, he told me he was going into town. He never came back and I never saw him again. I was extremely sorry about what I'd said to him. I went into town and questioned a number of other hobos, hoping that someone had seen him or knew where he was, but no one could tell me. Apparently, he had just gone on his way. I had come to love him as a brother and I deeply regretted my outburst. I should have just kept my opinions to myself.

It seemed to me that Lee was caught in a spiritual battle. He was trying to do the right thing in a bad situation. He was struggling with his soul because he didn't have enough faith to give himself up and trust God with the consequences. I knew that what I'd said to him about trusting God was basically right, but I still wished I hadn't said it. Lee was like family to me. After a few days of searching, however, there was simply no sign of him and I was forced to give up and let him go.

"What is it with this 'God thing'?" I thought to myself. "Everywhere I go, his name comes up!" The subject of God seemed to be haunting me and causing problems for me wherever I went. Keith and Johnny, the two cops who used to live next door to me, had clearly believed in God. Candace had always held to a belief in God. My next-door neighbor in Memphis had been a pastor. In each case I had resisted their talk about God and the older I got, the more vehemently I defended my atheistic stance. Now my best friend, Lee, had tried to get me to repent and trust in God, and I had pushed him away. God was causing me so many difficulties!

But I still didn't buy all this God talk. I genuinely believed that spirituality was a crutch people depended on because they were too lazy to plan and prepare for life like I did. I thought that having faith – if it meant depending on some unseen reality – was a ludicrous thing to do. Hope and faith that was unseen was not logical to me, though I knew that Grandma had gone to her grave with this hope.

"If God is real," I thought as I packed my camping gear and prepared to leave New Mexico, "then why has no one seen him? Why is he hiding? *Where* is he hiding?" In truth, I felt I had more evidence to make a case for Satan's existence than God's. Satan you could clearly see; you only had to look at people – the robbers, thieves, liars, rapists, conmen, murderers and pedophiles who populated society. Wasn't that proof, if it was needed, of the existence of evil? Furthermore, I reasoned, "Why would God allow a person to be born blind or an innocent newborn baby to have a handicap? Why are some people deaf and tormented? How can God allow a man to make nine babies with a woman and then simply walk out of their lives? Why would a good God make it possible for the birds to survive without hustling, yet make it a daily chore for man?"

Grandma always used to speak about the "heroes" of the Bible – men like Moses, Paul and David. But from my reading of Scripture, they all just looked like criminals to me. "Moses killed a man in Egypt," I had told Lee. "Paul arranged the murder of innocent people," I had informed the pastor in Memphis. "David was a sadist and a womanizer," I had pointed out to Father Clements. This was how I saw it. Solomon was a ladies' man; Adam and Eve were deceivers. And Jesus? He was simply a fraud –the biggest fraud of all time. Logic told me that nothing could rise again once it was dead. When a tree dies, it's gone forever; when a leaf falls, it's finished; when we die, that is it. "My grandmother never rose again and she was a big believer in God and the resurrection," I thought. "She worshipped him every day, but her faith didn't put food on the table; government checks put food on the table."

I accepted that evil was a part of life, but I just couldn't accept that God was. To me, evil was a good thing because it made me want to survive. My world thrived on strength and logic, but all this talk of goodness was weak. If you tied and bound me with a piece of rope, I could not escape simply by believing I'd be free. I could not be freed through faith – I would need to apply logic and arrive at a method for releasing myself, based on what was binding me and its weaknesses. This was the method I had used to beat Father Clements at chess and to steal from his safe. I learnt all about a thing's weakness and then took advantage of it. I had exploited Valerie's weakness back in that New Orleans jail. I was able to pass the psychological exam for the Police Department by focusing on its weaknesses. I was able to steal cars due to the inherent weakness in their security.

Strength and survivability come through thoughtfulness. What you call scheming, I called thinking; what you call theft, I called an opportunity; what you call lying, I called awareness; what you call robbing, I called living; what you call cheating, I called wisdom. If God existed, there would be no evil. If God existed, I would not be able to take advantage of people. I was convinced that there was a way around every obstacle and it was not through faith.

"People all around the world fill churches and pray every Sunday," I reasoned, "yet the biggest sinners in the world are the people in those churches!" I knew that a lot of turmoil and backstabbing takes place in church. "These people bicker with each other every seven days like clockwork," I told myself. "Why would anyone want to be part of that?" I had often gone into a church, but only to get some free money. I knew that if you went to a pastor and played on his love and emotions, then generally, *voila!* – you'd get free money! Sure, whenever I did this I would regret it, but not because of God. My regret was that these fools didn't see it coming.

As far as I was concerned, my bad deeds were simply the result of a giant chain reaction. If I did bad things to someone today, it was only because someone did bad things to someone else yesterday. We devour one another daily, just like lizards eat insects and lizards are eaten by birds, and so on. People, I decided, were the ultimate predators – heartless, fakers, liars and cheats. Once, in Nashville, I even saw a blind man steal. A little girl visited the concession stand he was operating in a hospital. She bought a fifty-cent bag of potato chips, handed the man one dollar, and he handed her twenty-five cents in return. You might say that was simply a mistake, but when I tried to give him fifty-five cents for a sixty-cent item, he knew I'd shortchanged him. I promptly stole an item from him in memory of that little girl.

Grandma always said to do the right thing, but my motto was, "If you do the right thing you will not survive." The "right thing" was whatever you needed to do to survive – and I was certain I was going to survive. Using the knowledge that Lee had imparted to me, I hopped the next train out of New Mexico. I would miss him a lot, but I *would* survive.

I hit him so hard on the head that I fractured his skull.

Chapter 12

Los Angeles, California – in the Gang

I
t must have been some time in 1989 when I headed out further west and arrived in Los Angeles, California. I arrived by train late morning and began to explore this vast city. I headed to the nearest bus station and struck up conversations with the locals, picking up as many tips as I could about where I could eat, sleep and bathe. As usual I located a mission downtown on the first night, then continued exploring the landscape the next day.

In the late eighties Los Angeles was full of gangs like the Crips, a large African-American gang who had been around since the end of the sixties, and the Reds. They were full of young men who wanted to be gangsters – robbing, shooting and fighting. Purely by coincidence, I ended up being connected to an up-and-coming gang who had about thirty members at that time. I wasn't interested in joining any gang, only in what I could get out of them, especially since they were a foul mixture of thieves, rapists, drug dealers, liars, swindlers and murderers.

It happened one day while I was sitting in a park. About ten members of this gang were throwing a football around nearby, laughing and swearing at each other and generally causing a disturbance. At one point, the football came into my vicinity, so I reached down and threw it back to one of the members. Immediately, however, he became indignant and belligerent towards me. He was young, about twenty years of age, six feet tall, but very well built, weighing around 200 pounds. He told me I had violated some kind of rule, which I didn't quite understand, and hurled a stream of abuse at me. I stayed calm and simply explained I meant no harm.

The seriousness of this incident escalated quickly, however, as the other gang members began to crowd around me, so I quickly got off the bench and made to leave. The first young guy yelled at me to stop and then the others joined in, shouting that I had disrespected their friend and something had to be done about it. Not even I wanted to take on ten guys in one go, so I tried very hard to defuse the situation, telling the guy I was very sorry, I should never have touched his ball and so on. I said I apologized if I had disrespected him in any way.

Apparently this wasn't good enough for him. He told me I had to fight him, hand to hand, to solve this problem. I was in a difficult situation. All these guys had circled around me, each of them swearing and cursing at me, desperate for the fight to kick off. I weighed up my options. I thought about running, but I was well and truly cornered. I asked this guy, if I won the fight, what would happen next. He told me if that happened, I could leave. He was a well-built specimen, but so was I and I knew I had some advantage over him due to my police self-defense training. In the end I agreed to fight him.

I was feeling very intimidated by his friends. Could I really believe his word? Would they simply let me leave if I floored this guy, or would they all take me on at once and give me a severe beating or even kill me? I had no choice, so I could only hope it would be a fair fight. As we moved into a small playground in the park I told myself, "This is just another challenge you must overcome, Robert." I wanted to win this battle and, hopefully, get out of Los Angeles in one piece as quickly as possible.

The young guy got into his fight stance and I got into mine. He came towards me swinging and yelling. I simply engaged him. We fought hard, hitting one another for about fifteen minutes, although it seemed like an hour. His face was pouring with blood and so was mine. Then, one of the other guys (who I learned later was the leader) stepped in and separated us, stopping the fight and telling us it was a draw. My nose was pouring blood, one of my eyes was swelling up, and I had several cuts to my jaw.

The leader asked me where I was from and where was I going. I told him I'd just arrived in town and wasn't looking for trouble. I learned his name was Jeff, a captain of this gang and third in command. He told me he could provide a place for me to sleep and eat that night. I agreed, reluctantly, though I didn't want to be drawn into this gang. I told myself that the first opportunity I had to get away from them, I'd take it.

We walked to an old, weather-beaten house about two blocks from the park. I was bleeding all over the place. I was scared because it crossed my mind that they were luring me back to their headquarters just to kill me, but with gang members all around me I couldn't see a chance to escape this insanity. As we arrived at the house, Jeff knocked on the door with a pre-arranged series of taps familiar to the occupants. The door opened and I could see another ten to fifteen members inside, some sitting on a sofa, others standing against the walls, others squatting on the floor. I was petrified. In the middle of the room was one guy working away, bagging up marijuana. Someone else was bagging cocaine, while another was giving stern orders to someone on the telephone. Another guy was cleaning a pistol. I could see these hoodlums were evil; they had their hands in all sorts of vices. I sat down on a sofa at the leader's request and simply observed. Then he went around the room questioning members about various tasks he'd given them, giving out more orders, and speaking with them as if he were the CEO of some company. When he'd finished checking on business he came and sat next to me.

"Would you like to make $100 to $200 a day?" he asked.

"How would that be possible?" I asked.

"Work for us as an enforcer," he replied.

I felt in no position to refuse his offer at that moment, with many pairs of dangerous eyes watching to see how I would respond, so I went along with the conversation. I asked him specifically what my duties would be, if I did it. He told me it was simple: go and collect overdue money and if the clients didn't have it, kick their butts. He told me that the guy I'd fought earlier had never lost a fight and even though I didn't beat him, I had not lost either. In other words, I was well qualified for the job and I'd make some easy money. I agreed to do as he asked, hoping that it would allow me an opportunity to escape.

He gave me a hundred-dollar bill, which he said was "a deposit", and then told me that after getting some sleep we would start working. He escorted me to one of the rear bedrooms and said he would see me in the morning. That night I laid on the bed and wondered how on earth I could get out of there. There was only one window in this bedroom and it was barred and locked. Outside the door was the constant sound of voices and the footsteps of other gang members. I was trapped. I lay still, thoughts buzzing around my head, and somehow fell asleep.

The next morning, I awoke to a tap on the door. It was the guy I had fought the previous day. I discovered he was known among his colleagues as "Killer". I saw that his face was badly swollen from my punches, especially around his eyes. I'd laid some good hits on his face. He spoke to me sternly and ordered me to come into the living-room. I dressed and entered the room a few minutes later to find Jeff speaking to the other gang members about their accounting practices. He wanted to keep track of where the sale of certain narcotics was taking place. I listened quietly until he paused and introduced me to all present.

The previous day he'd asked me if I went by any nickname and I'd told him I was known as "Tiger". I wasn't, of course, but it seemed that they all had gang names that sounded violent or threatening, so I made it up on the spot. He never once asked my real name, nor any questions of a personal nature. He seemed confident I wasn't a police officer or anyone off limits to their operations. I thought about that hundred-dollar bill in my pocket. At that moment I was a little more willing than the night before to "review" this gang organization and see what I could make out of it.

Although I'd had no intention of joining a gang or becoming

an enforcer, I figured I would run with this opportunity, at least for a while, and go along with what Jeff wanted. He gave me my assignments and I began to go out into the neighborhood to collect the gang's debts. Mostly, these debts were drug related. I visited people who had bought narcotics from the gang and were selling them on to others or maybe using them themselves. I visited the buyers at their places of work, on college campuses, anywhere I could find them. My method was simple. I would show no compassion or sympathy. Either they handed over the money they owed or I gave them a beating.

One day, I visited a local playground to find a guy who owed them $1,000. He was playing on the swings with his five-year-old child and his wife was standing nearby. It was a picture of domestic harmony. I walked up to him and told him I needed to speak with him privately. He agreed and as we talked, a few feet away from the swings, I ordered him to pay up. Of course he told me, as many people did, that he didn't have the money and wouldn't have it for a couple of weeks. Without warning, I struck him in his face, hard. He fell to the ground as his wife ran towards him screaming. Then I walked over to his child, pulled a pistol out and yelled to this guy, "Now I'm going to ask you again. When will you have the money?" He and his wife pleaded with me not to kill their child. He said he would get all the money in twelve hours. I stood there with my pistol pressed to his young child's head for almost a minute before deciding to give him a chance to get the money.

This incident gives some insight into my frame of mind at that time and how low I had sunk. I had just wanted to be by myself, to be left alone to live my life, to avoid captivity, but now I had been sucked into this evil racket and, despite myself, had risen to the role. If I was going to be an enforcer, then I would be the best enforcer in the city. Looking back, I don't think I ever really intended to pull that trigger. It was more of a shock tactic, designed to get a result and quickly. But maybe, knowing the animal that I was back then, just maybe I could have, if I thought it was necessary. After this incident my notoriety spread throughout the area. Everyone who owed the gang money suddenly started paying up. People had begun to hear about my ruthlessness.

Jeff had given me a book containing the business transactions I was to collect on. I severely beat anyone who didn't pay on time according to that book. One day I went to collect from some guy and beat him so badly that I broke his jaw, which had to be wired. I also hit him so hard on the head that I fractured his skull. Instead of paying up like everyone else, though, he promptly went to the police and told them what had happened. Later I discovered that he had given them a good description of me, so good that I could be in danger of being caught. I went to talk to Jeff about this problem and he advised me to get out of town and run to Seattle, Washington, where an offshoot operation of the gang was based. I told him I would.

As I left Los Angeles, however, I didn't go to Seattle. Instead I caught a bus going east. I was simply too scared. The gang members constantly ran the risk of being arrested for carrying drugs or for their violent behavior, but none of them were fugitives from justice like me. I had a lot more to lose. I realized that I had crossed a line once again. I had made myself vulnerable to capture and I could not allow it to happen again. I left California and headed east to Florida.

*A new person had been
born... conniving, wise, and
certainly able to conquer
many challenges.*

Chapter 13

Florida and the Great Smoky Mountains – Back in the Woods

round 1990, I arrived in Jacksonville, Florida. I had now been on the run for around eleven years and was into my thirties. My twenties were wasted – that person had died long ago. A new person had been born... conniving, wise, and certainly able to conquer many challenges. I arrived in Florida and followed my usual modus operandi: I set up a new car-stealing business.

It's never hard to find shady characters, lurking around the periphery of decent society, if you know where to look – and I was good at finding them. Within a couple of hours of hitting Jacksonville I had located a fence to whom I could sell stolen automobile parts and I had the right connections in place. Florida was not the perfect place to steal cars, because there were so many elderly retirees there and old people tended to be much more safety conscious about their vehicles. But I was able to steal them anyway – it just took a little more time.

My car-stealing enterprise took off and was soon going well, so I rented a nice apartment. I wasn't planning on settling down again, I just wanted to make enough money to buy camping equipment. Almost every time I set up camp somewhere, events conspired against me and I was forced to abandon my gear. I blamed God for this, since it always seemed to have some connection with him. "The next time I buy camping equipment," I vowed, "I am not leaving it behind."

After a few months of apartment living, it was time to hit the woods. It's hard to explain the affinity I now felt with the outdoors. If I was careful, I could have easily lived in a small, anonymous apartment somewhere in a quiet back street, under an assumed identity and been perfectly safe. But I was addicted to the woods. It was the only place where I felt absolutely safe.

The area around Jacksonville and the northeast part of the state was teeming with woods and I located a good spot in Osceola National Forest. Once settled into my camp, I felt peaceful again. Upon every return to the forest I became more efficient at hunting than before. Hunting was second nature to me now. I also became quite good at identifying various plants, leaves and trees.

In Florida, there are black bears living in the forests. I ran across them several times, especially in the summer months. Florida also has cougars, which I encountered once or twice. I made sure I was well equipped with special hunting knives, should I need to defend myself, but fortunately I never had to take on a cougar. Knowing that they populated the forest made me feel somewhat nervous going to sleep each night, but I devised what I believed to be a good defense system against these big cats. I had learned from years of observing wild game that if an animal knows a human has been in a particular area before them, they will avoid it. So in order to "mark" my territory and ward off intruders I regularly urinated around the perimeter of my camp. The cougars never bothered me.

Snakes were another native of the Florida woods, but they never gave me any trouble. Snakes feel your vibration as you're walking through the woods and they move away from you. I liked to find the occasional snake to capture and eat, however – especially rattlesnake, which was a delicacy in New Orleans. A supermarket called Schwegmanns I used to visit sold rattlesnake in cans. It was tasty and full of protein.

As well as the wild game I hunted, I supplemented my diet with various other things. Grubs were easy to find. They didn't taste good, but again, they were filled with protein. I gathered various kinds of berries which were my only source of carbohydrates. I learned that you don't need to eat a lot of carbohydrates in order to live. Ninety-eight per cent of my diet was meat. I always had extremely low percentages of body fat when I lived in the woods, probably around seven to eight per cent. In the absence of carbohydrates, the body switches to burning fat to provide energy. After a week of eating only protein I could literally feel this process kick in. When my body began burning fat for fuel I experienced a kind of euphoric high.

I remained in the woods of northeast Florida for two more years until, in 1992, I developed another physical problem. This time it was some kind of skin problem. It started small, with patches of red skin appearing here and there, but eventually my whole body looked like a strawberry and I knew I had to venture into Jacksonville to get help. This skin problem troubled me more than the eye problem I'd had. It itched and burned badly. I thought it must have been caused by something I'd touched or perhaps eaten.

Emerging from the forest, I sought out the nearest hospital and presented myself in the emergency department. The doctor couldn't figure out what was causing the problem, but said he would give me some medication to apply to my skin. I came into contact with so many different trees and plants, I figured it was just a reaction to something. As I waited in the hospital pharmacy for the medicine, I saw a fellow I knew from a couple of years before. As we talked, he mentioned that he'd just arrived from Georgia a couple of days ago. During our conversation he told me he had seen Lee and that he was currently in Atlanta, living with some other guys in the woods just outside the city. When he said that, I thought he might be speaking of another Lee, but he insisted, "No, I remember you guys used to hang out together." I inquired a little more as to the exact location and he gave me enough information to zero in on the site.

I'd not seen Lee for a couple of years, of course, but I'd constantly missed his company, so I decided I would try to find him. After collecting my medication I began hitch-hiking towards Atlanta. It took me about three days to get there. I headed for the bus station and asked around. Some guys were able to direct me to the area where Lee was staying, but when I arrived he was already gone. Everyone told me he had headed north. I'd missed him and I was really disappointed.

I hitch-hiked back to Jacksonville and went to the mission to find the guy who'd originally told me about Lee. This guy was a true hobo. In other words, he ate, slept and lived on trains. I had around fifty dollars in my pocket, so I told this guy I was going to purchase a beeper. I said I'd keep it for a couple of months and gave him the number, telling him that if he saw Lee to give him the number and tell him to get in touch. I realized, after buying the pager, that it would require charging or some new batteries eventually. I had no access to power in the woods, so the best I could do was hope that he might connect with Lee again in the next couple of weeks and get him to contact me. It was a real long shot, but I wanted desperately to see Lee again. A week or so went by and the beeper gradually lost power. Sadly, Lee never called me.

Back in the woods, I discovered that I needed to move my camp location. A crew of engineers had come into the area and were clearing a piece of land just a couple of miles away. If I lit a campfire I would instantly give away my location and draw unwanted attention, so I looked for a new spot about a mile north. As I moved through the woods searching for a site, I happened upon an old, weekend campsite. Lying on the ground, I noticed an old newspaper from Charlotte, North Carolina. I sat down to read it. In the classified section there was an ad about an organization in North Carolina who were looking for individuals with survival skills to work at a camp. I wondered whether I could do what I loved doing – living in the woods – but actually get paid for it. I made an instant decision to go to North Carolina.

According to my earlier vow, this time I carried my camping equipment with me. It took me about two weeks to hitch-hike to North Carolina from Florida. I tried to hop a couple of trains on a few different occasions, but I was not as good as Lee and it seemed as though all the trains I hopped were going the wrong way. Eventually, when I was near to the location, I stopped and called the number on the advertisement to speak to someone about the position. The person on the other end of the phone was keen for me to come and be interviewed, but mentioned that, of course, I would need to provide identification and they routinely did a background check. My heart sank as I realized I couldn't go for this job. It was silly of me to think I could get a job working around young adults and kids without a background check. "Why didn't I think of that?" I chastised myself.

Since I had taken the trouble to hitch all the way to North Carolina, I thought I might as well set up camp there, so I decided to stay in Charlotte and search for an appropriate wooded area.

* * *

There were a lot of woods outside of Charlotte. The forests there almost looked like Canada. The day before I entered the woods, I went into downtown Charlotte to see the city. It was a nice place that seemed to consist primarily of banks. There were banks on every other street corner. But there were only one or two missions in the town, so it was not a good place for a homeless traveler.

As I walked around town, I stopped at the local Greyhound bus station, as was my habit, to speak to the other travelers and glean any useful information. Not for the first time, something struck me as funny. "If the police departments around the country are serious about catching fugitives," I thought, "then there are three places they will always find them – missions, day labor offices and bus stations!" I had frequented these places in every single place I'd visited. Fugitives always hang around bus stations because generally they are going somewhere!

I chatted to the hobos who were gathered there and one of the guys said he'd just arrived in town from Columbia, South Carolina, where the Rail Yard Police had almost busted him and a couple of fellows last week. He mentioned that one of the guys he'd been traveling with was named Lee. Surprised and excited, I asked him to describe this guy and he gave an accurate description of my old friend. Immediately I prepared to go to Columbia, South Carolina to search for him.

I hopped a train to South Carolina. When I arrived, I searched the local missions and bus stations and inquired about Lee. One guy said he'd seen Lee the day before I arrived. For the next three days I searched for him, but there was no sign of him. I looked diligently for him, but never found him. I didn't like Columbia that much, so I decided to leave and move on.

I decided to go back into the woods again – back to the Great Smokies. Some years had passed since my run-in with the rangers there. The Smokies are so vast that I figured I could get lost easily enough. I traveled to a city called Gatlinburg and washed and waxed cars for a whole month to get enough money to gather the necessary supplies and then headed into the mountains. As I journeyed deep into the Smoky Mountains I thought to myself, "Most people would be scared to death to do this." To walk away from society is a serious endeavor. To sleep and eat in an environment filled with all sorts of wild animals sounds ludicrous to most ordinary people. But I had learned so much about this environment that it was like home to me. At first, I did it out of necessity, but now I enjoyed every moment of it.

In due course I found what seemed to be the perfect place to set up, in a clearing among the trees. I unpacked my gear, set it out as I was accustomed to doing, and settled down for a night of relaxation. During my previous visit to the Smokies I had noticed that at a certain time of night, a small plane would fly overhead, circling the woods. On this night, I heard the same plane. I had to assume that it was the State Police, patrolling the mountains from the air. I also guessed that they could easily be equipped with infrared cameras that could identify heat sources – the heat from campfires, in other words – so anytime I heard that plane, I put out my fire. In the still of the forest I could hear them approaching thirty minutes before they arrived in my area.

One day, after being in the Smokies for a few months, I was

out hunting deer. I was gone for about three or four hours and when I returned to camp, I saw that some of my prized gear was gone. I looked around my campsite in shock. After studying the scene a while, I knew the forest rangers had not done this. I also knew that a bear couldn't have done it either – unless bears are in the habit of taking coffee pots. I figured another squatter was probably in the area and had stumbled across my camp. "Somebody has stolen my stuff," I fumed. I was angry because it was obvious that the gear had not been abandoned.

I searched the perimeter around my camp carefully to pick up the intruder's tracks. In about ten minutes I had located them and was following his trail. As I tracked his steps, I picked up my compass and made trace markings to find my way back, since I didn't know how long I would be walking. After approximately one mile I saw the camp. I figured some guy had just taken my gear. Subtly, I surveyed the campsite and slowly approached it, careful to stay near the bushes. I saw a guy cooking food with my gear nearby.

After making sure he was alone, I entered the camp. I surmised he probably didn't have a weapon. I confronted him and told him he had taken my gear. He didn't own up to it straight away, but then told me that he'd thought the camp was abandoned. "Sure you did," I said sarcastically, knowing full well he was lying. He began arguing with me, asking me to prove the gear was mine, while I simply began collecting what was mine. It's difficult to prove you own something when you're living in the woods – it's not like you keep the receipts. As I went to pick up my coffee pot, he tried to grab my arm. We fought like dogs for about ten minutes. Eventually I got the better of him and he backed off, at least enough for me to retrieve my gear, and I left.

When I got back to my camp, I collected all my other gear together and decided to get myself well away from the area. It was sheer coincidence, I decided, that he had set up camp so close to me, but I didn't want any more hassle from him. Eventually, I found another site some three or four miles from there and normal life resumed.

Living outdoors takes its toll on your body and soon more physical problems began to develop. Getting sick was the only thing that would cause me to leave the woods. This time my stomach hurt terribly. I decided it was time to get help, but as I prepared to go and find the nearest doctor, I got sicker and could not leave that day. I went to bed that evening and slept all night and half of the next day. The next evening, I felt much better. I decided I must have eaten some spoiled meat. Feeling ill made me realize that I really needed to be close to a bigger city. Gatlinburg was a small place. I needed to be near somewhere that had better medical facilities, should I need them.

I reviewed my options and decided that the best state I'd lived in was Florida. There were woods all over the place – plenty of options to choose from – and good facilities all around them. So I hopped a train going south and eventually reached Jacksonville once again. At the local mission, I struck up a conversation with a guy who said he was going to Tampa. I thought I might go there as well, since I had no particular place to go, so we traveled together by train. But he was nothing like my old friend, Lee.

* * *

I arrived in Tampa in around 1996 and soon parted ways with my traveling companion. I found the local mission and began to explore the seedy parts of town. At the mission I bumped into a guy named Sam. He struck me as a bit unusual, not your average hobo type, but I couldn't put my finger on what was different about him. That is, until one day when I happened to see him in the street, just before he went into the mission for the evening meal and bed.

Sam was sitting in a brand-new car that he'd parked up the street, a safe distance from the mission. Inside he was changing out of some pretty fancy clothes into something more typical of a traveler. I was puzzled. "What's this guy doing staying in a place for the destitute and homeless?" I wondered. I couldn't figure out his game. I was curious and so I watched him carry on this routine for a couple more days. He would park two blocks from the mission, change out of his nice clothes, and then come in and fool everyone. The counselors at the mission would have kicked him out instantly, had they known.

After I'd seen him make his little "transformation" a few times, I decided to ask him outright what he was up to. As he sat outside one night, smoking a cigarette, I struck up a conversation with him and he knew I was on to his deceitfulness. He told me he was a "player" and got paid for "entertaining" women. He was basically a conman, but he also told me that, unbelievably, he'd fathered fifteen children in Tampa and didn't pay child support for any of them.

"Women…" he said to me. "All you have to do is speak smoothly, love them and then take their money."

"But if you're doing so well," I asked, "why don't you just get an apartment?"

"I've got two apartments," he replied, "but some of these women are looking for me and I need to wait until things cool off."

He looked at me. "Do you smoke?" he asked.

"Only good cigars," I replied.

He reached into his pocket and produced a fifty-dollar bill.

"Here," he said. "Go buy a good cigar."

I took the fifty-dollar bill, thinking it was a really nice gift. We talked some more and he divulged his *modus operandi*. He targeted lonely, rich women and nearly always had success. Before he'd gotten into this con game, however, I gathered he had worked as a gigolo – a male prostitute.

"Robert," he said, looking me up and down, "you're not a bad-looking guy. All you got to do is talk smoothly and entertain the women and you'll get paid well."

Those fifty dollars made me listen to his theory. After he'd explained a bit more I decided there was some merit in it. Though I was frequently troubled by guilt and shame, my atheistic view of life meant that neither scruples nor morals prevented me from doing what I wanted to do. It sounded good to me, so I asked him how I could get started. He told me to be ready at nine o'clock the next morning and he would show me how to make some serious money.

In the morning I slid into Sam's incredibly stylish car and he drove me downtown to meet a middle-aged lady who ran a hotel. Effectively, she was a Madam who arranged for guys to entertain bored, wealthy ladies. She was well connected; some of Tampa's richest women were her clients. She looked me over, gave me $300, and told me to go and buy some decent clothes.

When I returned that evening she informed me that she knew I'd only spent half of what she'd given me. I wondered how she knew! Hell, I wanted to keep some of that money for myself. I tried to make an excuse, but she shrugged it off. "Well, anyway, you are ready now," she said. Then she called in her assistant, a guy, who took me up to one of the hotel rooms and gave me a shave and a nice, clean haircut. Afterwards, he informed me that in the room down the hall a lady was waiting for me. I really didn't know what to make of all this, but I was in it for whatever it was worth.

A few minutes later, I went to this room and found a lady of around fifty sitting waiting. After I had "entertained" her, she got up and left. As she went I followed her out of the room and watched her stop by the front desk. She handed the Madam an envelope which was immediately placed under the counter where no one could see it, then they said their goodbyes. After she'd left, I spoke to my new "pimp" and she handed me $200. I was amazed. $200 for an hour's work wasn't bad. Then she informed me that I had actually made $350, but she was deducting the $150 I was supposed to spend on clothes.

Just then, Sam appeared and walked up to the desk. He and the Madam discussed an incoming client he was to entertain. After they'd finished talking, he asked me if I liked the job and I told him of course I did. A new chapter had begun. Twice a week I met this one lady and made around $700 a week, just for entertaining her. Eventually, I had enough money to rent my own apartment and I enjoyed this new scheme immensely.

One day, however, I saw a lovely young woman at the local gas station and struck up a conversation with her. Her name was Crystal.

We seemed to hit it off immediately and eventually exchanged phone numbers. I called her that same evening. She was a quiet woman, something like Candace. We talked every night and ultimately got close.

As my relationship with Crystal grew, I wanted to spend more and more time with her and I frequented the hotel less. This caused a problem for the pimp lady. Apparently the rich lady was refusing to see anyone but me and my absence was damaging the Madam's income. Sam informed me that the rich lady was paying her $800 per visit in order to see me exclusively, out of which she would pay me my $350. She was one of the Madam's most important clients.

One day the pimp lady came over to my apartment and asked me outright what it would take for me to stop seeing Crystal. At that point, I knew I was finished with the business. I was in love with Crystal. I told the Madam that I quit, and she was understandably upset. She offered me more money, but I refused. After a while I moved to another apartment near Crystal's place and I never returned to the hotel again.

Crystal and I became very intimate. She worked at a local bank and made good money. She was a decent and honorable lady. Eventually she became pregnant. This would be my fourth child on the road.

Crystal wanted to get married, and her family insisted we marry. Her mother was a Christian and a pillar of the local church. Her father was Associate Pastor at the same church. I told Crystal we would get married, but all the while I knew it was impossible. I was a fugitive and Crystal had no idea about my past.

As time went on and I continued to put off the issue of marriage, Crystal and I began having problems. She wanted us to be married immediately, but I was constantly stalling, making one excuse after another. Eventually, her father and I had some words about this and the end result of the conversation was that he clearly hated my guts. I didn't blame him, though. She was his only daughter and did not deserve to be treated unfairly.

Eventually, as much as it broke my heart, I realized that this relationship was caught in a Catch 22: I couldn't get married because I was a fugitive, yet I couldn't not get married if I wanted to keep Crystal. I would have to create fake identification in order to get married and this in itself could leave me vulnerable to exposure. In the end I decided that Crystal didn't deserve someone like me and I certainly didn't deserve her. I didn't know how to break the news to her, so I packed my bags and left Tampa.

I used all of my intelligence, logic, and reasoning to survive... to survive by any means necessary.

Chapter 14

Tallahassee and Miami, Florida – Stealing Hearts

It was about 1998 when I moved to Tallahassee, Florida. I was far enough way from Tampa, so I looked for and eventually found an apartment and pondered my next move. I had inadvertently used so many people by now, and I had lost virtually all feeling for humankind. I was more inclined to be nice to an animal than a person. My lifestyle had turned me into an emotional husk, devoid of compassion.

I had been a fugitive for nineteen years now and this process had turned me into a machine of hate. I felt as though I was one with Satan. I was his best student, his prize pupil, his gold standard. I had no feelings; I was just evil on two legs. Although I have described many events in this book, I can't begin to tell about all the bad things I've done in my life. The Bible and God meant nothing to me. I could swear, using God's name, and it meant absolutely nothing. I was like steel – cold and hard. I was a danger to others and to myself.

Gradually, I had moved away from stealing cars and onto something much worse. I had no soul! I used all of my intelligence, logic and reasoning to survive – to survive by any means necessary. I had fathered four children whilst on the run, but I never saw any of them. I thought that perhaps the mothers of those babies loved me, but I did not return their love.

There was a park in Tallahassee that the locals frequented. It wasn't a large park, but it was very popular and I would often

130

hang out there. Ironically, it was not far from the Tallahassee Police Department. While sitting on a park bench one day, I saw an attractive young lady walking around the park. I watched her go around the park a couple of times and at one point, she returned to her car. She drove a nice Jaguar. As she walked past the bench I was sitting on, I asked if I could walk with her.

"This is a free park," she replied. "Walk where you like, but not with me."

"This could be a challenge," I thought to myself and jumped off the bench, hurrying to catch up with her. I was a cocky, arrogant, evil person with no sense of modesty and because I liked the look of this girl, I told myself she would be mine. Modesty was for the weak, I thought. My philosophy was to go out there and take what I wanted in life. As I caught up with her, she and I traded light insults with each other. She played right into my hands. Even a conversation consisting of insults is a conversation. As we traded barbs, she began to jog. I jogged right along with her. Then the jogging became a run and I ran with her.

After a good 400-yard run, we both stopped by her vehicle, gasping for air, and then we laughed. The conversation suddenly became more light-hearted. She mentioned she was a personal trainer at a local gym and inquired if I was into fitness. I told her I was and she observed that I was in pretty good physical condition, as if I lifted weights. I told her I had been working out for over twenty years. The conversation drew to a close as she said she had to go, but she gave me her phone number. A few days later, I called her and during our conversation she mentioned that the local YMCA was looking for a personal trainer. She thought I should look into this, so that evening I did. A few days later I began working at the YMCA.

One day while training, I met another lady named Monique. She was a good-looking woman. Monique was, as she put it, slightly overweight, but that didn't bother me. Every day, we chatted about physical fitness and health. Eventually, she hired me to be her personal trainer. After a few weeks, however, I didn't charge her for our sessions. We became partners in love.

I truly cared for Monique. I know I've written that I cared about every woman I ever met, but this time it was truly different. It was different because we became good friends first. We shared many things in life. Even the things we didn't like about each other were still respected. I discovered eventually that she worked in a local office, having just graduated from college. For a long while we didn't talk much about what each of us had done or were doing in life – it just didn't seem to matter that much. Monique was about twenty-seven years old and she assumed I was about thirty. In fact, I was about forty-three years old. Her mother and father, who lived in another state, were only about five years older than me. Monique and I continued our relationship and it grew stronger each day.

Since I was a body-builder (and looked the part), many guys asked me what I did to look that way. The hard life I'd led had toughened and hardened my body and my biceps were huge for a man my size. Most of the guys assumed I was taking steroids, but in fact, I was not. The constant exercise regime I kept up in the woods, combined with an outdoor lifestyle where I would walk for miles every day, had contributed to my physical shape.

One guy, David, was obsessed with building his muscles. He would come in every day and bug me about getting him some steroids. After many weeks of him nagging me, I finally told him I would. I got the steroids from a friend at another gym and gave them to him, coaching him on how to train while taking them. David was about five feet, eleven inches and 275 pounds when he started taking the steroids. In three months, he gained about 50 pounds of muscle. He was on his way.

Unfortunately, David told many other people about my ability to get steroids and in time all the guys were bugging me to get supplies for them. Since they seemed to be in such high demand, I decided to start selling them. My mark-up on the steroids brought in decent money and I soon became well known as a steroid dealer among the hardcore fitness guys. I sold steroids to all sorts of people and continued to build an enviable reputation as a good trainer. My success became so widely known in fitness circles that I began training semi-professional body-builders. I attended various contests with my pupils and they did quite well.

Monique knew nothing about my steroid proprietorship. I kept it hidden very well. We fell deeply in love and, inevitably, the subject of marriage came up. This was the fifth time I'd been engaged and, honestly, I wanted to make the marriage possible in some way. She had never been married before and it was a deep desire within her. I thought I could manufacture some false identification to make it happen for her, but I got sidetracked with business matters. My steroid business was growing so quickly I couldn't keep up with it.

One day a professional body-builder came from Miami to see me. He offered me a sweet deal. This guy was all over national body-building magazines in the late nineties and was among the top ten body-builders in the nation. I was very impressed with him. When he came into the gym one evening, everyone asked for his autograph. Most of the honest fitness people wondered why he was there. His reason for showing up was, of course, because he knew I had good access to "gear" (the street name for steroids), plus he wanted to work with me because I was known as a hard trainer. My sessions were notoriously difficult and not for the weak. I would get very irritated training regular guys; I wanted to work with professionals.

This guy offered to relocate me to Miami so that I could train him personally and supply him with steroids. He said he would make me wealthy. I knew this was a possibility, given his high profile and, as usual, I was hungry to be successful in my new "vocation". I began to talk to Monique about it, telling her that Miami was the place for us to be. She had no problem with relocating. She told me she was tired of Tallahassee. Just before we moved, she informed me she was pregnant. This would be my fifth child as a fugitive. Monique had no idea I was wanted.

We moved to Miami in 1999 and found a place to rent on Miami Beach. It was small, but sufficient for our needs. Before we left I told Monique I'd acquired a job at a prestigious gym. I was not lying. I trained and worked out at one of the best gyms in Miami. Some of my contacts from Tallahassee also moved to Miami a couple of months after I did, so that I could continue training them.

I worked closely with the body-building star and supplied him with massive amounts of drugs frequently linked with the sport: testosterone, D-Bol, Winstrol, Anavar and Insulin. His body was a walking chemistry experiment. I learned so much about steroids and their ancillary drugs that the fitness buffs started calling me "Doc". I threw myself into studying my topic and excelled at it, just as I had always done. I knew how steroids could affect the body, positively or negatively. I understood their impact at a cellular level, what pathways they took through the body and how long they stayed in one's system. I think even today, I might know more about steroids than most doctors.

In the first couple of months in Miami I made plenty of money, but then a problem developed. The main guy I trained and a few others I supplied began asking for credit because they needed a bit more time to pay. They were regular, reliable customers, so I gave them credit, but this turned out to be a big mistake. I obtained around $10,000 worth of steroids from my supplier and then these guys were very slow in paying me. My supplier quickly became edgy and then his edginess turned nasty. Before long he was issuing death threats and the situation had become really serious. Steroids are harder to get hold of than regular drugs. Big people, serious criminals, are involved behind the scenes – people who would think nothing of wiping out some small-time dealer if he was interfering with their cash flow.

I used to carry my supply of steroids around with me, concealed in a large black bag. Monique always asked me why I lugged this bag around with me and constantly kept it close, but I fobbed her off with some excuse. Not only did I want to keep a watch on those drugs, but in the back of my mind I thought that if the police ever kicked in our apartment door, it would protect Monique from being implicated.

Monique had gotten a modest job at an insurance company and we were barely making ends meet. Our financial situation caused a strain on our relationship. She was pregnant, working and trying to pay the bills, but my loaning out credit was bankrupting us. Monique couldn't keep up. One day, my supplier told me I had three days to come up with $15,000 or else. I put pressure on my customers, saying that they must pay me immediately, but they threatened to go to the police. I was caught between a rock and a hard place. At this point, Monique was about six months pregnant and things looked very bleak for us.

Meanwhile, her mother and father were pressuring her to return home. I didn't blame them. A pregnant woman doesn't need the kind of pressure she was experiencing. Monique's mom was a Christian and so was Monique. She never knew I was an atheist. Monique would often ask me to go to church with her and I constantly made excuses until she stopped asking. Her mom had a big problem with the fact that I didn't attend church with her daughter, and every time she called I would overhear the two of them discussing our bad situation. I gathered that her mom must be hitting her hard with the God talk, because afterwards she would be flipping through her Bible.

One day as I arrived home from the gym, I saw a police car parked outside of our apartment. I wondered what was going on. Immediately I was ready to run. I could easily have left, there and then, and headed for the woods, but something stopped me. I was struggling with my feelings for Monique. I felt the same way about her as I'd felt about Candace twenty years earlier. I really loved her. Plus, of all the children I'd fathered, I wanted this baby badly.

Taking a deep breath, I entered our apartment and looked around. I saw a police officer standing in our bedroom. Monique was packing a bag. She told me she was leaving. I tried to speak to her and convince her not to leave, but she wouldn't have it. I assumed this was the reason the police were present – she just wanted to leave without discussing it with me. Maybe she was afraid of how I might react, even though she had nothing to fear from me. It seemed she had figured I would force her to talk, but she was determined to go. After a few more minutes, she got her bag and left. The cop and I talked about relationships a little and after a while he left. I was devastated. I cried for the first time in years. I hadn't cried like this since Candace left me in Toronto. "This God crap has done it to me again," I told myself. "I found love; now it's gone again."

Most atheists are people who simply don't believe there is a deity, a force higher than humanity. They believe that life on earth was triggered randomly and that we live our lives to the best of our ability, then we die, period. Atheists don't tend to hate other people's religion, they just don't want the religious views of others forced upon them. But I had gone further than this. I had developed a great hatred for the subject of God and the mention of the Christian religion incensed me. I believed that the very concept of God was flawed, yet this "abstract" concept, as I saw it, had managed to hurt me many times. "God" had influenced situations in my life through people that I loved and the result was they were torn away from me. God had come into the situation once again and now Monique was gone.

I cried for the remainder of the day after Monique left. That first night, it rained very hard for the first time in a while and it seemed symptomatic of my life. My pain, coupled with the dark, dreary night made my outlook seem bleak indeed. I blamed God for my circumstances, or rather, the belief in God of those I loved. I vowed that the next person who got close to me – whether it was a woman like Monique, a friend like Lee, or even a priest like Father Clements – I would prove to them that all religion was foolishness. I vowed to myself that I would learn all I could about the Bible and its teachings. My motivation was to seek out its inherent contradictions, to disprove it, to expose its false ideals. I was going to look at all of the concepts and philosophies relating to God and his existence as tenaciously as I had tackled the subject of wilderness survival. I was determined to expose Christianity for the charade it was.

Monique's absence in my life turned another page in my journey. I was particularly upset that I might not see my child when it was born. I'd had five children in twenty years and not one of them was in my life. After meeting Monique I had begun to enjoy life outside of the woods and often felt like a normal person. I was still a fugitive, I knew, but after twenty years I was beginning to feel that the authorities would never catch me. Monique called me every week or so, but I could tell in her voice she was no longer in love with me. After a few months I deduced that there was someone new in her life. This really upset me. Some other guy would raise my child, and my child would call some stranger "Daddy".

I tried to handle the difficult situation I was in by pressuring the people who owed me money. Some paid a little, but others still paid nothing. The pressures on me were so great, that I resorted to threatening some of my clients. In response to this, some of them went to the police and reported that I sold drugs out of the gym. At that point I had to stop all my illegal activities. One day I observed the police parked outside of the gym, questioning various members about steroids. Things were getting hot and it looked as though I would have to leave Miami – mainly because my suppliers were continuing their threats to hurt me. But just when I was getting ready to run again, the body-builder who'd persuaded me to move there came through with just enough money to keep my suppliers off me. I cleared up my debt with them and avoided a dangerous situation. But I was finished as a dealer. They would never trust me with that much gear again.

I continued to work at the gym as a trainer and some time later met another lady. It seemed I had no problem in meeting attractive ladies – I just never managed to keep them. This girl's name was Marie and we lived together for a short time. I was attracted to her simply because of her gorgeous looks, but she was the most challenging person I ever had a relationship with. In many ways she was similar in character to me: cold, methodical and calculating. I guess you could say I finally met my match. We argued constantly because she continually suspected me of being unfaithful to her. Anything I said to her was doubted and double-checked. Eventually I began to hate Marie, even though we stayed together. Every time I walked out the door, she suspected something was going on between me and other women, and I was unable to convince her I could be trusted.

One day as I left the house, Marie followed me (I was unaware she was monitoring my tracks). I went to sit in the local coffee shop and suddenly noticed her watching me from her vehicle in the parking lot across the street. At that point, I knew I had to get away from her permanently. I had been seduced by her good looks, but it had been weak of me and a mistake. A woman this paranoid was exactly the kind of person who was capable of reporting me to the authorities. I had become careless. It was time to leave Miami and go and explore another city.

You might say a squirrel or some animal or something else could have moved the rock, but I was convinced God was speaking to me.

Chapter 15

Back to Memphis, Tennessee – a Miracle

I finally moved back to Memphis, Tennessee, during the early part of 2001. Although I didn't know it at the time, after years of moving from place to place, Memphis would be the last city I would live in before returning to New Orleans.

I was still thinking like a fugitive. *I've got to get back into the woods* was the only thought on my mind. After the ups and downs of life in normal civilization, I couldn't wait to be back in the wild. I sold anything and everything I had that was sellable to raise cash to buy camping gear. As I stood in the camping equipment store some weeks later, I could not help but laugh at myself. I had gone from being a woodsman to a sharp-dressed, hustling ladies' man, back to being a woodsman in a matter of a few years. One minute I had no girlfriend, the next I had several girlfriends; one minute I was broke, the next I was wealthy... and then I was broke again. It was a strange life. But I was nothing if not adaptable.

While I was in Memphis, I called my old girlfriend Veronica, the mother of my daughter – my third child on the road. By this time my daughter was fifteen years old – old enough to think and act independently – so when I asked Veronica if I could see her, she asked her daughter and the answer came back, "Yes." I can hardly describe the feelings I had going to visit her for the first time – a mixture of excitement and sheer trepidation – but our meeting went well and the two of us really got along. She was not bitter towards me, though I could not have blamed her if she was. She said she just wanted her dad to be in her life. Her words cut me like a knife. After all, wasn't that all I had ever wanted? To have my father in my life as a role model – the father I never had?

After a couple of visits I was ready to set up camp in some nearby woods. I told my daughter that I was getting an apartment in Memphis and would visit her regularly. I had no money to get an apartment, of course, and didn't intend to do anything other than camp in the woods, but I wanted to give her some sense of stability, to know that I would be around for her.

I found a place to camp in a densely wooded area surrounding Memphis. As outdoor living goes, it was by far the worst place I ever lived. The fleas and gnats were notorious and I was constantly being bitten. I dealt with it as best I could. I set out my camp taking all the usual precautions and arranged my gear in an orderly and methodical fashion. I had a small supply of cans of soup and potted meat, but intended to resume hunting quite quickly. In this part of the woods there were no deer – only birds, squirrels and rabbits. I didn't have any trouble snaring and hunting these animals. I loved rabbit. Cooked properly, it's delicious – especially rabbit soup.

During this time in 2001, I lived like a true woodsman. I could sit down in my camp, look around the woods and tell if any animal was in the vicinity. I could listen and identify any type of bird. I could identify various tracks and tell if that animal had been walking, running or hunting. I was at one with nature. I could eat things a goat wouldn't eat! I could lay down any place in the forest and it was as good as a comfortable bed to me. By now I was very different from the jittery, nervous man who had laid down to sleep in the Canadian forest. Now I was tenacious, logical, cold and aware.

At night there was nothing to do except think. I often looked up into the sky at night and admired the stars and moon, trying to identify different groups of stars and planets, and as I did I would think of all the people I'd met and recall my relationships with them. My old friend Lee often came into my thoughts and I wondered if he was OK. Had he eventually given himself up? Had he continued to run? Did he think about me, like I thought about him? Was he comfortable, coping with life? Lee and so many others flashed across my mind. So many places, so many games and cons, so many victims, so many girlfriends and children. I even remembered with fondness my family of bird friends back in Canada. If they were still alive, they would be great-grandparents right about now. But mostly I congratulated myself for surviving and not giving up. I was proud of the fact that I had risen to this challenge. For more than twenty years I had successfully evaded the authorities. As I slowly fell asleep under the stars of Tennessee, I thought of my Grandma. In my mind I kissed her on the cheek before drifting off.

During the third or fourth week in the woods of Tennessee, a man walked straight into my camp. It was about 6 a.m. and I was drinking my morning cup of coffee. He was a vagrant and a loner who was out wandering in the woods. He startled me as I heard him walking through the brush, but my police training quickly told me that he posed no threat. Upon discovering me he approached somewhat nervously and then spoke to me. He told me he had been walking in the woods and had lost his way. After a few minutes of small talk he mentioned he was on the run. He said he didn't know what to do and remarked on how comfortable and well maintained my camp was. I told him I had been living in the woods for years. I offered him some coffee and we talked about some of his problems. He refused to speak specifically about his fugitive status, and I didn't press him, but he told me he'd only been running for a couple of weeks. He was both astounded and interested to know how I could live like this, so I told him how I'd started on this journey and how, in time, I'd learned to live off the land. I could see he was mentally trying to absorb everything I said. We talked for hours about my journey.

I could see that this guy had no place to go and little clue about wild living. I felt sorry for him, so I told him he could share my camp for a little while. He had a sleeping bag and a few canned goods, but that was it. I realized that, due to his lack of knowledge, he was totally unprepared for this kind of life. Gratefully, he set up his sleeping bag a few feet from mine and we continued to talk about strategies for survival in the woods. Materially, anyone could prepare for living in the forest, but mentally the forest would test any man's courage. In the forest you don't have the benefit of light, people, safety or security. You are literally in danger from the moment you enter – not only physically from wild animals, but in danger of losing your mind – and this is something you have to accept early on and learn to live with. Often, during those first difficult nights in Canada, I was so scared that I contemplated putting my gun to my head and pulling the trigger. That's how difficult a challenge it is.

I assured this fellow that this was no game. I expounded in great detail that he would have to give up his mother, father, sister and brother. There would be no more aunts, uncles or friends. He had to give up his identity in its totality, lose all of his loved ones, and accept the reality that in the future, anyone he loved or who loved him would also have to be held lightly and probably sacrificed for the sake of freedom. I related to him all that I had been through – the sorrows, pain and loneliness. I explained that the sorrow was something so deep that one could find himself contemplating suicide.

After I'd explained to him what life would be like for years to come, he began crying. He cried loud and deep. I didn't say anything else, I just let him cry. He cried like I had cried back in New Orleans. He stood up and stretched his arms to the sky, then he let out a primal, heart-rending scream. He screamed for what seemed like minutes. Afterwards, he dropped to his knees, put his head down, clasped his hands in prayer, and fell to the ground. I didn't try to comfort him in any way. It appeared my experiences had brought him to the reality and seriousness of his own situation.

I got out of my sleeping bag, walked over to his weak, sorrowful body, and looked down on him. He was curled up in a fetal position and in deep emotional pain. I lightly placed my hand on his shoulder and spoke to him. "If you are crying now, what will your future look like?" I continued to talk, educating him on the realities of fugitive living, telling about things he would encounter that he wouldn't see or expect. I wasn't trying to be heartless. I wanted him to understand that this decision he was making required something inside I didn't believe he possessed. In order to survive in the wild you had to become animal-like: heartless, without compassion, ruthless, tenacious, resolved, diligent, reacting without thinking or regret. As only an animal knows nature, so must you. I continued to tell him, "You must be calculating, focused and a devourer. Kill or be killed; conquer or be conquered; win or be defeated." After I had finished my speech, he lay stretched out on the ground and began praying to God out loud. When I heard him crying out to God, I returned to my sleeping bag. I knew then just how weak he was. I was in no mood to hear this God foolishness again.

I awoke in the morning around 5 a.m. and noticed him packing up his few belongings and preparing to leave. I watched as he left the camp. I said nothing, but simply watched him walk out through the forest. For a few days afterwards I thought about this fellow. I knew my uncompromising account of life in the wild had brought home to him the stark reality he faced. I was sure that he didn't have what it took to survive like that, and was certain that he went home and turned himself in – especially after I had dissected his thoughts and plans and shown him how small his chances of success were.

For the next few weeks I hunted, ate, lived and conquered the forest. Weakness, hesitation and uncertainty were not options for me. I lived and thrived in the woods. But little did I know, the very feelings I had described to that poor guy – the tidal wave-like emotions I thought I had conquered long ago – were about to come and ambush me for a second time. It was a completely shocking turn of events and I was both unsuspecting and unprepared. It began one day when I woke up feeling very strange. I couldn't figure out what it was, but I felt strange for the entire day. I had an ominous feeling in my gut, the kind you get when you feel as though something bad is about to happen, even when there is no apparent reason for it. I kept wondering what it was that was setting off my instinctive alarm system. Was I going to get hurt or die?

For a couple of days, nothing happened. Then, all of a sudden, as this feeling washed over me once more, I was finally able to describe it. I was tired. So, so *tired*. I was tired of running, tired of hiding, tired of being unable to live normally like other people. Feelings swept over me that pushed me to end it all, to end my life. I was never going to give myself up to the authorities – thirty-plus years in a penitentiary at the age of forty-six was a death sentence. I would never see the light of day again – so that left only one option. The only way out was suicide. I had faced and conquered numerous challenges in my life. I had beaten the odds time and time again, somehow prevailing, though the circumstances were stacked against me. But I didn't want to face any more challenges. I had been to many places and done many things, but now the world was dull to me. After all was said and done, I had to admit my life was still unfulfilled. Every chance of happiness that had come my way, I had blown. I was finished.

The mind at twenty-three years of age is so different from the mind at forty-six years of age. You become much wiser, clearer and more knowledgeable about many things in life and this dramatically alters your perspective. At twenty-three I was arrogant enough to think I was invincible and immortal. Now I was a middle-aged man, still in good shape, but a little slower in my run, a little weaker in my walk, and a whole lot more in touch with my mortality. I didn't think I possessed the mental fortitude to go on with this.

For days I struggled with suicidal thoughts. My desire to stop running, to simply put an end to it all, battled against my will to survive. My will to survive was powerful – it was all I had – but the desire to commit suicide was powerful also. The way I saw it, everything of worth in my life had evaporated: brothers and sisters, sons and daughters, a home and a career – all lost. And I had lost myself in the process. *I didn't know who I was any more.* In the process of running I had assumed many different identities. Every person I met in each new city knew me by a different name. I had been Michael, Ken, Bob, Jermaine, Charles, Fred and Keith. But not only had I used a different name, I had created a different personality for each of these identities. No wonder I couldn't remember who I actually was.

One night, as I lay down to sleep, I experienced a dream –

a very real dream. In it my Grandma was debating with the devil. Grandma insisted that, in time, I would see the error of my ways and repent. The devil insisted that I would not. God was sitting in the middle, listening to this argument. The devil made his case before God and informed him that I was a soldier of evil. Grandma, however, refused to give up on me. She was certain that I would repent and be redeemed. The argument continued for a long time. Every time the devil offered proof of my evil deeds, my Grandma fought back with something good I had done. They went back and forth until God finally made a decision. He concluded that I was evil and said he would deal with me. On hearing this, Grandma begged God to deliver her to Satan rather than me. God asked her if she was sure. She said she was. At this point I woke up. I was yelling for my Grandma with tears in my eyes. I didn't want her to go to hell. I couldn't sleep for the remainder of the night. The dream was so vivid that for many minutes I was convinced it had actually taken place.

I sat looking at the weird shadows the moon cast through the trees and thought of Grandma, her pretty smile and warm heart. I thought of her constant hope for me and my siblings – that one day she would see us in heaven. Grandma was the first woman I ever loved. People say that if you want to know how a man will love, look at his first love. I can still feel her rough, scaly hands touching my neck. She worked hard as a cook in a restaurant before she began raising us. Physically she was tough, but spiritually she was soft. There was nothing, I mean nothing, which she would not do for us.

This dream stirred something in me long forgotten. I was transported back to see the Robert of the 1970s; the me that I knew in the distant past. I relived the banter I'd always enjoyed with my brothers and the jokes we told one another. I relived the tag football games we'd played in the streets, the cotton candy and candied apples we always enjoyed at Pontchartrain Beach. I thought of the many days we wrestled and "play" fought with each other. I thought of Grandma's homemade preserves, her perfect sunny-side eggs and her smoky ham. I thought of her at the sewing machine, sewing a shirt a week for each of us. I recalled my sisters' stupid laughs when they pillow fought among each other. I thought of our old bunk beds with the multicolored quilts, of our small, shotgun house with its squeaking floors and leaking roof. I remembered the neighborhood cat I would feed each morning. I thought of our one little television with no channel knobs. I recalled our living-room sofa, so hard and so cold. I thought of our dogs, Spot and Butch, chasing some stranger as he walked by. I remembered our old-fashioned clothes dryer that I would hand crank every day. I thought about Henry, Charles and James, my childhood friends. I simply thought of home. I sat there all night trying to figure out whether I had been dreaming or if there really was a debate going on in heaven about my future.

As the next day dawned I continued to ponder all these thoughts. What could this dream mean? Was it, in fact, a dream at all? As I sat there, I looked up at a tree close by. I had looked at this particular tree many times over previous weeks because it had an unusual feature. Near the top it had a kind of bulb attached to its trunk and at certain times of the day one of its four sides would open. Later it would be closed again and another side of it might open. It struck me as being quite odd and I'd not seen anything similar in all my time in the forest. I looked at it again this morning and said to myself sarcastically, "If the side on the north is open by tomorrow morning, then God must be real." As soon as I'd said these words, I checked myself. "What am I saying?!" I could scarcely believe the thought had passed through my mind. I was an atheist, after all. God was non-existent!

I went to sleep that night and awoke the next morning, chastising myself for my stupidity. But I looked up at the tree to see that the north-facing side of the bulb had opened. "A coincidence," I thought. Then I said, defiantly, "OK then, if tomorrow morning the south side of that bulb is open, then God is real." I didn't have to wait until the next morning. A few hours later the south-facing side of the bulb had opened. A shiver went down my spine. Was I going crazy? I didn't believe in God, but could it be that God, through his creation, was telling me he was real? I knew from my study of the

Bible that in the past a prophet had performed a similar kind of test with God. He'd placed a fleece on the ground overnight, where he knew it would gather dew. He determined that if, the next morning, the ground was covered with dew, but the fleece remained dry, he would know God was speaking directly to him.

To me, this seemed like a conclusive test. Only a genuine miracle could produce a result like that. So I decided to conduct another, more rigorous test myself. I took off both my shoes, placed them at the foot of the tree and said out loud, "If I wake up tomorrow and there is a single leaf in the left shoe, then God exists." The next morning there was a single leaf was in my left shoe. Because I was stubborn and not prepared to let go of my beliefs easily, I tried another test. After all, many leaves could have fallen off that tree during the night and one of them could easily have landed in my left shoe. It could still be a coincidence! So the next night I placed an upturned can on the floor and put a small stone next to it. "In the morning," I said, "if the stone is underneath the can, then God exists." When I awoke next morning the pebble was gone. I was too frightened to actually look underneath the can. You might say a squirrel or some animal or something else could have moved the rock, but I was convinced God was speaking to me.

I left that can exactly where it was and refused to disturb it. As far as I know, it is still sitting there now with the stone underneath it. "Let someone else witness that miracle," I told myself. "I'm not moving it!" Thoughts of my Grandma's faith and God flashed through my head and I dropped to my knees and began to pray. I spoke to God and quickly and sincerely apologized to him for every bad thing I had ever said to him or about him. I was terrified in the truest sense of the word. A holy fear came over me that I find it difficult to describe. Perhaps you can understand something of how scared I was if I tell you I later discovered I had urinated on myself. Only the experience of deep terror can make one lose control of one's bodily functions. I was being confronted by the reality of God's presence – a God who can make rocks move when they are not supposed to. You can call me crazy, but God had got my attention.

God spoke to me and told me exactly what I had to do with my life next. I was to quit running, surrender my life to him and, ultimately, surrender myself to the authorities, leaving the consequences in his hands. I had no option but to obey him. I got myself together enough to leave the woods and headed immediately into downtown Memphis, straight to the nearest phone booth. I was thinking only about God revealing himself to me, the overwhelming sense of awe I felt at his presence, and of reconnecting with the family I had missed for all these years. I would attempt to find someone, anyone, and then I would give myself up. I got through to directory assistance and began reciting the names of my brothers and sisters. Eventually the operator was able to give me the number of my youngest sister, Thecla. I had not heard or seen her since she was about twelve years old. With my heart in my mouth I dialed her number. Within a few rings she answered the phone.

"Thecla?"

"Who is this?" she asked.

"It's your oldest brother, Robert," I said.

"Who? Robert? I don't have a brother named Rob…" Her voice trailed off and there was a brief silence. Then it came to her.

"Robert! This is Robert?" she screamed.

"Yes," I replied.

She couldn't believe it was me. She kept asking me over and over, "Are you really Robert, my oldest brother?" I assured her it was me. After speaking for another ten minutes or so, during which I described our old house and everything in it, she was convinced. Then I asked her if she would do something for me.

"Would you be able to gather the family together at your house in two days' time?" I asked. "I'm going to give myself up."

She started crying. My little sister and I had not seen one another in twenty-two years and we both missed each other. She asked me if I was sure and I told her yes, because God had told me to do this – words I never thought I would hear myself saying. I told her when I would be arriving in New Orleans and then hung up the telephone.

It was then that I looked down and noticed that I had no shoes on. My encounter with God in the woods had frightened me so much that I had taken off barefoot without even realizing it. I returned to my campsite, still terrified, and sat down a safe distance away from "the can". I watched that can as if it was God himself. It seemed to represent something from another world. I had challenged God to prove his existence to me and he had – several times. I watched the can for hours, contemplating my discovery. God *really was there*, yet I had ignored him, even hated him, my whole life. Occasionally a leaf rustled or a twig broke and fell from a nearby tree and made me jump, but I was transfixed. I couldn't tear myself away, not even to eat or drink. I could do nothing but think about God.

As darkness approached, I lit a fire and saw the glow slightly illuminating the can. As the flames danced, for a moment it looked as if the can was moving. I closed my eyes and covered my head, staying under cover for the rest of the night. Sleep was hard to come by and I didn't drift off until around 3 a.m. Even then, I only slept because of exhaustion. My body felt like lead. I could hardly move and I couldn't speak or open my mouth. I awoke at 6 a.m. and exited my tent, being careful not to look at the can. I gathered only those items necessary to get me to New Orleans.

"Someone else can have my equipment," I thought. This would be the last time I left the woods, terrified, much as I had been the day I entered them.

As I walked in, every one of them started crying, hugging me and thanking God.

Chapter 16

New Orleans – Homebound

T wo days later, most of my brothers and sisters gathered at Thecla's house. As I walked in, every one of them started crying, hugging me and thanking God. It was a very emotional scene. We cried, talked, hugged and loved each other. The emotions generated by twenty-two years of absence were extremely powerful. After we had spent some time greeting one another, I announced to them all that I was going to give myself up. "They can do whatever they want to do to me," I said. "I'm not running any more."

It was clear that all my brothers and sisters still believed in Grandma's God – a loving God who works miracles for those who love and belong to him. They told me that if I'd turned my life over to him, then maybe he had other plans for me rather than a life in prison. Each of them said they would take the next day off work and accompany me to the Police Station downtown. I was no longer scared. I was simply resolved. One of my brothers said he knew something dramatic must have happened to me to bring me to this. All I knew was that the "rock and can" incident in the woods was enough for me. God had proved himself. There was no doubt in my mind any longer. I had evaded capture for more than twenty-two years, during which time not even thoughts of suicide or the most extreme hardship had motivated me to give myself up. God had done what no one and nothing else could. He had persuaded me to give in. Before bed, one of my brothers came and asked me if I was very sure this was what I wanted to do. "Definitely," I told him.

The next morning we arrived en masse at the District Attorney's office. We walked into the building, which was just across the street from the courthouse and two blocks from the Police Department. "Can I help you?" the receptionist asked politely.

"I need to see the District Attorney," I replied.

She sensed the urgency of the situation and returned with the District Attorney. I provided my name, the crime charged against me, and announced I was giving myself up after twenty-two years as a fugitive. He looked as though this was some kind of joke. I assured him it was not.

He walked over to a nearby computer and examined the files. All my family members were crying except my brother Tony, who was an ex-military man and a no-nonsense type. Minutes later the DA returned. He said there was no record on the computer of any Robert Davis who was wanted. By now, we had begun to attract some attention and a number of detectives were milling around in our vicinity, presumably ready to arrest me as soon as my details were verified. But after searching his databank for a second time the DA could still find no record of my crime. "Mr. Davis," he said, "according to my records, you are not wanted."

I insisted that I was. I was ready for this nightmare to end as quickly as possible. The DA said he would research my situation in the morning. I told him that I was ready for jail now. Calmly he replied, "If you are wanted, I'm not worried about you running. If you were going to run, you wouldn't have given yourself up." After that he took my sister's address and phone number and told me to come back at 9 a.m. the next day.

The whole situation was extremely puzzling to me. I couldn't figure out what was going on or why the District Attorney had no record of me on his system. I returned with my family at 9 a.m. the next morning to speak to him. The DA told me he'd had to search the police basement archives to find any details about my case. Apparently, at the time when I'd fled, most case reporting was done manually and later, when an extensive computer system was introduced, not every case going back years was transferred onto it. He placed a paper file on the desk in front of me. It was thick and looked old and dusty. In it were details of various investigations that had been carried out in an attempt to find and apprehend me over a twenty-two year period. Also in the file were details of the charges filed against me and other information dating back to 1979. Then he told me we would have to walk across the street to the courthouse and see what the Judge wanted to do about this. He said this was an incredibly unusual case for him. On the one hand, I was a fugitive. On the other hand, I had surrendered.

In due course we found ourselves in Section C of the Orleans Parish District Courthouse, the department where the case had been assigned back in 1979. The original judge had retired, unsurprisingly, but Section C still had jurisdiction of the case. As we walked in, a trial was in session. The Judge was a lady and the DA approached her. He apologized profusely for interrupting the proceedings and said that he urgently needed to speak with her. She agreed and put the trial into recess. After a brief private discussion, I was called into the Judge's chambers. She told me she was going to allow me to leave in the custody of my sister, but requested that I return promptly to handle the situation. I assured her and the District Attorney that I was not going to run any more. Like the DA, she also believed that I would not flee.

* * *

A couple of weeks later, on March 3, 2002, I returned to the Section C Courthouse for my hearing. Judge Hunter, the lady I'd met, was presiding. Every one of the bailiffs and police officers present knew by now who I was and what I was in for. Some of the cops there hadn't even been born when I became a fugitive. My brother, Tony, accompanied me. When I left New Orleans in 1979 he was working at a local hospital. Now that I'd returned, I discovered he'd spent twenty years in the US Army. It felt like we'd spent a lifetime apart. The military had left its mark on Tony. He was a very straightforward person who did not believe in pity or weakness.

As we sat together on the courthouse pews, waiting for my case to come up, all kinds of people from other sections came in to catch a glimpse of me. I felt that some of them were trying to shame or embarrass me with their stares. "If they knew what I'd been through," I thought, "they wouldn't waste their time." These tactics could not embarrass me. Tony leaned over to me at one point and shared a disturbing rumor. "Robert, I'm not sure, but I think I heard that the Judge's daughter or some relative of hers was raped a while ago. If that's true, then she is probably going to throw the book at you. She can't possibly be lenient with someone who did what you did after what happened to her relative." I looked at him in shock. I knew he was trying to prepare me for the worst. I didn't know if this rumor was true, but I studied the Judge's face, trying to detect anything that would give me an indication of her mood.

I didn't know what God had planned for me and maybe this was some kind of test to see if I really was willing to surrender myself to him and leave my fate in his hands – just like I'd told Lee to. But I was resolved to let him have his way, come what may, and I addressed the devil under my breath: "Satan, I know you want me to run out of this courtroom and flee again, but I am not running any more. My spirit is not running any more. My soul is content with long years in prison or even death." I thought long and hard about my current situation, but I knew that everyone I'd ever known who loved me enough to tell me the truth would be telling me to stay. Father Clements back in Chicago would have said, "Make the right move," like when we played chess. Lee would have said, "Ride it out," like when we rode those bumpy trains. My Grandma, that pastor in Memphis, and all the people who cared about me would have told me to deal with this. And even if they had not, *I was prepared to deal with it.*

Over the years I had cursed God. I had cursed anything associated with God. But now I had given my life over to him. I had surrendered my strength and now I could feel his strength – a power greater than any I had felt before. I knew the Bible well because I had studied it in order to disprove God, but he had proven himself to me in a way I could understand. Now I had to put my faith in him. I recalled various biblical characters and their own challenges of faith, how they were tested under pressure and yet stood strong. Just like the apostle Paul had to defend himself before the council, I would stand. Like Moses who was called to stand on Mount Sinai and proclaim the commandments of God in the face of an unbelieving people, I would stand. Like Noah, whom God called to believe that the impossible would happen, I would believe. I had been to hell and back in order to come to the point where I knew God was real, that he wanted my life to mean something. No prison term was going to turn me away from him now. I had lived through the valley of the shadow of death for twenty-two years. Satan had no hold on me any more.

As I sat in the courtroom, I closed my eyes to pray. For about twenty minutes I talked to God silently. Tony didn't interrupt me. He must have known I was praying. My prayers took a similar line to those of Jonah, asking God to relieve me of this problem I was facing. I knew from my reading of the Bible that God always says we must believe first. Believe, have faith, and you can tell this mountain to move from here to there and it will move, Jesus had said. I believed that if God could speak to me through a pebble and a can, then he could do anything he wanted for me.

Just then I felt Tony nudge my leg. I had been so engrossed in prayer that I hadn't heard my name being called to stand before the Judge. I stood and took my place. Here I am, I thought, standing before the Judge's seat, with the seal of justice emblazoned on the wall behind; standing on these two legs that have carried me countless miles through the wilderness. Here I am, staring into the face of justice with eyes that have seen many horrors and witnessed many things. Now it is all up to God. What happens to me is in his hands and his alone.

"I'm Robert Davis, your honor," I said.

She reached across her desk for my file. It was easy to see among the others, thick and tarnished by years of wear. She looked at the papers and reports intently and with obvious amazement. Standing before her was a man who'd been a cop around the time she was in grade school; a man who was living in the woods around the time she was in college. After a few minutes of reading, she turned and looked at me. The first thing she asked me was where I had been all these years. I told her I had been living in the woods in various states and Canada. She asked me how I ate and I told her off the land. She asked me if I was ever incarcerated while I was on the run. I answered, "No."

In the meantime, my court-appointed attorney was speaking with the two District Attorneys who were there to prosecute me. Apparently, the District Attorneys had already made up their minds as to what should become of me. As my attorney and one of the District Attorneys approached the bench, scenes of my Grandma flashed through my mind. Thoughts of God and his power were also vivid in my mind and, though in a very real sense I was at my most vulnerable, spiritually I felt totally at peace.

The Judge addressed me: "Mr. Davis, I understand that you do not wish for a trial."

"That's right, your honor," I replied. "I am guilty of this crime and I am guilty of many crimes."

"Do you understand the consequences associated with this confession?" she inquired.

"Yes, your honor," I stated.

"Has anyone forced or convinced you to make this confession?"

"No, your honor."

She reached for my file once again and was quiet for several minutes more while she reread the facts of my case. Eventually she looked up, stared me right in the eyes and said, "I am going to sentence you to two and one-half years in the state penitentiary in Angola."

I did not flinch. I was not scared. I simply replied, "Yes, your honor."

But a split second later I heard her say, "But…"

I looked at her, amazed. There was more? An extraordinary, astonishing statement followed her "But".

"But… I will suspend this sentence and place you on two years' probation," she said.

I could hardly believe my ears. I would not be sent to prison! As she spoke those words I looked up to heaven and to this day, I swear I heard a voice from above, so loud and clear I thought everyone in the courthouse must have heard it:

"Good job, Robert. I am pleased with you."

Some discussion between the Judge and all the attorneys followed, during which I stood still, silently praying, thanking God for his mercy to me. Even when Judge Hunter turned back to me and said I was free to go, I remained motionless. I could tell from her voice that she had been touched by my story. I don't think that she pitied me, but she understood what an ordeal I had lived through and obviously felt *that* punishment was enough in itself – living cut off from my family for a quarter of a century, running scared, never able to be myself.

"Mr. Davis, you are free," she repeated.

My heart was beating as rapidly as if she had sentenced me to death. I had truly believed that this lady would show me no mercy, but God's mercy had prevailed. He deserved all the glory for this miracle. As I thanked her and turned to walk away, the last thing I heard her say to me was, "Good luck, Mr. Davis."

As I walked down the aisle of the courtroom, heading for the exit, an elderly woman who looked strikingly like Grandma reached out and touched my arm. She smiled at me and said, "Jesus loves you very much." I looked over at my brother Tony and could see the joy on his face. We hugged each other lovingly. I turned to scan the courtroom one more time. The same people who previously seemed to be trying to embarrass me were smiling now. Humbly, I returned the smile.

* * *

As my brother and I exited the court, a couple of police officers standing outside shook my hand. My brother hurriedly searched for a telephone to call the family and tell them what had happened.

Meanwhile, I spoke to my attorney. I thanked him for his service and he wished me luck. As he walked away to handle some other case, I went over to a window in the courthouse and looked outside. I wanted to be alone. While I waited for Tony to return I looked out over the city of New Orleans. It was bustling with activity. People were milling about, going about their day, unaware of and indifferent to what was happening inside the courthouse. "Most of those people don't know how precious life is," I whispered to myself. "They don't know the importance of family and friends."

I stood there a very different person to the Robert Davis of old. I was not cocky, nor did I feel victorious. I was a humble man. For Judge Hunter to release me was a great blessing. She'd had every legal right to show no leniency whatsoever and give me thirty years in prison. I will forever be grateful for her actions. She showed me something I had not shown to many others: compassion. She had shown mercy to a man who had a habit of making bad decisions. If I'd been called to account for all the crimes I'd committed in my life, there was little doubt I would be facing life imprisonment. But here I stood, a free man at last. I realized for the first time that true freedom can only come as a man admits everything he has done in the past, no matter how vile or insane it may be, and throws himself on the mercy of God. Not every man gets a chance for such redemption. Judge Hunter gave me that chance, through God. I wished I could see her outside of court to thank her, but I know she felt my gratitude through my humility before her bench.

As I stood there, looking out of the courtroom window, a bird alighted on the ledge. I looked at it and said, "Go and fly to my friend Lee and tell him the good news." The bird flew away. I closed my eyes again to pray to God. I must have been there for several more minutes and when I opened my eyes my brother was standing next to me. He had not wanted to disturb my prayers. Although he was a tough guy on the surface, Tony was a compassionate man. He had stood by me through this whole ordeal. Earlier, before court, we had asked our other family members not to come with us to the courthouse. I didn't feel I could endure them all crying as I stood before the judge and was sentenced to jail. I only permitted Tony to come with me because I knew he was strong and could deal with this situation. Tony turned to me. "Let's go home," he said.

As we left the court, I told Tony that we should have some coffee. He said there was a small coffee-shop downstairs. "No," I said. "Let's go down to the French Quarter and have some *real* coffee." I wanted to visit my favorite coffee shop, Café du Monde. I had not tasted their coffee in years. As we reached the coffee-house and sat together, sipping our drinks, I thanked God for this amazing moment. I never imagined that I would sit as a free man ever again, in my home town, with my brother, smiling and talking. I looked at the many tourists crowding the streets and thanked God again. That day I thanked him over and over, so much that I thought, if it were possible, he must be tired of hearing it.

Later we went to visit a relative's house and there we celebrated together as a family. I was not caught up in the celebration as much as I should have been. I found a moment where I could slip outside and get some air while the party continued. I spotted a small grocery store about one hundred yards down the street, so I walked to the store and bought myself a Chunky® – my favorite candy bar. I devoured that candy and it was the best I ever tasted! Afterwards I returned to the party. I didn't think anyone noticed that I'd gone.

Back at the party, I was about to receive a surprise blessing. As I re-entered the room, over in one corner I spotted a young man who looked to be in his early twenties. He looked strikingly like I did at that age. My mind raced as I turned over possibilities and then I came to the conclusion: could that young man be my son? I wasn't certain that he was, but my gut feeling told me this was my son, Jaren. I walked over to him. Taking a deep breath, I asked, somewhat nervously, "Are you my son, Jaren?"

He didn't answer me with words. Instead he opened his arms and embraced me. We hugged each other for what seemed like hours. I didn't want to let go of him.

As I wondered what to say to him next, he pre-empted my thoughts: "Dad, everything is alright."

I embraced him again and whispered in his ear, "Son, I'm sorry. I'm sorry I wasn't in your life all these years."

Over in the corner I saw a little girl staring at me. Jaren explained this was my granddaughter and that she had a sister. Two granddaughters! I couldn't believe it. I beckoned for the little girl to come to me. Adorably, she just beckoned for me to come to her. I figured she had more than earned that right, since I'd been out of her life for all these years. So I went over and picked her up, hugging her tightly. Tears filled my eyes. A few moments later I felt a gentle touch on my leg. It was my other granddaughter. I had these two little girls in my life now. It seemed like an impossible miracle.

Seeing these little girls' innocence reminded me of Valerie, the young lady I'd victimized; the act which had started this whole charade. Earlier that day in court, my brother and I wondered if Valerie was present. I felt sure that she was, though I couldn't see her. I even wondered, after I was released, whether she might get in touch with me. I wished that she would, because I just wanted to apologize to her. I wanted to ask for her forgiveness and tell her how sorry I was. I wanted to tell her that the 23-year-old man she had encountered had been low-down, dirty, corrupt and so wrong to do the things he did. That person was dead now.

My thoughts were interrupted as one of my granddaughters asked me what kind of flower was in a pot she'd seen nearby. I told her what it was and she smiled. My son, who was now twenty-four years old, walked up to join us. We hugged and held each other and said how much we'd missed each other. I apologized to him for not being in his life when he really needed me. He was very understanding.

Needless to say, this was one of the best days of my life, with my brothers, my sisters, my son and my granddaughters. Life was bliss. On top of it all, I had a chance to start again, to be myself and not hide behind some false identity.

God was truly with me. He had permitted me to experience a miracle. I went to bed that night feeling very, very grateful. I still found it hard to believe that I could walk out of the front door and down the street and no one would bother me; no one was looking for me.

The next morning, my sister came to me and asked, "Are you ready?"

"For what?" I asked.

"You don't have any identification," she informed me. "We need to get started on it."

I had forgotten that I had no identification, no social security card, nothing. I had been used to carrying a fake ID or none at all. I realized I needed proper identification to function in the real world once again. It took a month for me to receive bona fide identification papers.

About two weeks after I was freed, three cars of police detectives came to my sister's house. I was not there, but they informed her they had a warrant for my arrest. My sister told them the warrant was old. This was true – there was a glitch in the computer system. The next morning, I straightened everything out, much to my relief.

For the next two years I worked out my probation, which involved making a regular visit each month to see my probation officer and receiving an unscheduled visit from him once a month. The first probation officer assigned to me was a nice guy, but after one month I was assigned another probation officer. This man appeared stern and was obviously a strict disciplinarian. I assumed he would probably give me a hard time. The first time I saw him he read my file and commented, "I see you were on the run for twenty-two years?"

"Yes," I responded.

He read some more and then looked me over. "I think you did the right thing," he told me. His name was Darryl Anderson. He and I got along well. He was the first man to treat me with any dignity since Father Clements. Like my brother, he had been in the military and was still in the Army Reserves. He didn't treat me any differently than anyone else on probation, but he knew I was a transformed man and respected me for it.

Looking back over my journey, I can see now that I never met an individual that God did not send my way. In some way, whether it was great or small, every person played a vital role in my eventual surrender to God and the authorities. Father Clements, my friend Lee, Judge Hunter, Darryl Anderson – they all played a role in my freedom.

Today, life is good and I have committed myself to serve God as best as I can. I suffer from some physical ailments such as arthritis, severe headaches and various skin problems, but life is *still* good. Doctors have told me that some of these conditions have been caused by rugged living over many years. It strikes me as funny that when you return to society, society's ailments come upon you! Upon my freedom and release it took me three weeks to start using a shower regularly, one month to sleep in a bed comfortably, two months to brush my hair, three months to answer to my real name and six months not to flinch at a police car. I still have some social adjustments to make, and I tend to enjoy being alone, but God is helping me. All of these issues pale into insignificance when I think about what God has done for me.

I spent a huge portion of my life running: running from God, running from the law, running from people and commitments, and most of all running from myself. But God never gave up on me, just as he will never give up on you. I am now totally free.

So can you be.

Chapter 17

Reflections – a Message to Young People

During my life I have lived through many different seasons and experienced a great many things. I have had a lot of time to reflect on the things I did, how I reacted in certain situations, how I arrived at the choices I made, and I have had the chance to process these in the light of Scripture, gaining God's perspective.

In the last section of this book, my aim is to impart the wisdom God has given me, having shown me the error of my ways, in the hope that others, having read my story, will learn to follow a better path. It is my earnest desire to lead others to the light, away from the despairing trail that I chose to follow. As you read, I hope you won't feel as though I am preaching to you. I just want you to absorb the wisdom of God and let him guide your life to become truly fruitful and filled with purpose.

A message to children and young people (aged 17 and under)

I wish for you all the riches of the world, good health, decent parents, strong family support, and that all your dreams come true. But please keep this in mind: all good things come from God. All success begins and ends with your love of God. Do you want success in life? Then first seek to have God at the center of it.

Respect your parents. Why? Not just because they gave birth to you (which is a miracle in itself) but also because God *joined* these two people together to make *you* – a special person. There is no other person on the face of the earth like you. But your strength and wisdom are drawn from your parents' experiences, wisdom and knowledge. I never knew a father, never heard his words of encouragement. I never felt the warm embrace of a mother or heard the words, "I love you." I and so many others in life were abandoned and cast away. What is love, true godly love? It's when an individual (like Christ) sacrifices their life for you. It's when a person puts their hopes and desires on hold to make possible your hopes and desires. This is what parents do. Godly parents will sacrifice their dreams in order to provide for your needs and give you a better future. Through you, however, their dreams can be realized. They will feel successful when you grow into a successful adult. They will lay down their lives so that you can live – just like Jesus did. So respect and honor their sacrifice by becoming all you can be in God.

As a young kid, I would often look at the other kids in my neighborhood and see them going to the movies together, picnicking in the park, playing games together and embracing one another. I would often wonder, "What did my siblings and I do to deserve this life without loving parents?" I look back on those days without love and affection and know now, without a shadow of doubt, that my life would have been different, had I benefited from loving, godly parents. Without embracing the love of your mother and father you will find it difficult to show love to others and your life will be empty of compassion. So love your parents. If you don't, there will be a hole in your life that you'll always find it difficult to fill.

As for your friends, never just *go with the crowd*. Any friend who attempts to guide you wrongly is a bad friend. Seek the counsel of others, such as your parents, adult relatives or even your pastor before agreeing to do anything questionable. When I was young, I would often persuade friends to assist me with stealing, but these were friends who had no parents to guide them lovingly, just like me.

I could never get friends who came from a stable home to discuss crime with me. Real friends will be more inclined to have fun, riding bikes together, playing games, going to movies. Friends who want to lead you astray are no friends at all. Listen to your conscience and do what you know to be right. Avoid speaking ill of others or calling them names, gossiping, plotting to do evil or stealing. You are a representative of your family. People will judge you, and them, on your character and morals, on your ethics and honor.

Cherish and appreciate your education. Waking up each morning to go to school may seem boring and tiresome now, but believe me, it will be worth it in the end. Without an education you will find it hard to discover your hidden potential, as well as experiencing difficulties in raising your future family. An education is directly connected to your future income, so every morning when you attend school, pray to God that he would give you knowledge and wisdom.

Be especially kind to your siblings. I have eight siblings, but am close to only two of them. Imagine the laughter, fun and love I've missed all these years. I miss the days of old when we were young and we would play, laugh and were close. I miss being a part of their lives now – the new nieces, nephews, husbands and wives. I diligently make every attempt to know them and their new lives, but somehow we're not all as close. We all need to hear God's admonishment to grow in love together.

Lastly, read your Bible and go to church and Bible meetings. Know God and receive his full blessing for your life. Romans 10:17 says, "Faith cometh by hearing, and hearing by the word of God" (KJV). We hear God by reading his Word. Whether you have a father in your life or not, realize today that God is your true Father. Almighty God has not abandoned you and will never do so, not matter what has happened in your life. If you have no father around to guide you, then seek the advice, love and companionship of an uncle or an older brother. You could also join an organization like the YMCA, your church youth group or The Big Brothers organization. But never give up or use the absence of a father as an excuse to fail.

Believe that God will take care of you, and he will do it! God does not lie, *that's a guarantee.*

You have seen my life as a youth, totally without merit, without honor, empty of love. Please, learn from my mistakes, love and honor God and be successful. Life is frequently difficult, but any obstacle can be overcome with God's help.

A message to young adults (aged 17–25)

You've got your driver's license now and maybe a car and a girlfriend or boyfriend. Maybe you're even working at your first job, earning your own money, or renting your first apartment and becoming more independent? This is a great achievement. You have become an adult. You've waited all your life for this moment: no more obeying Mom and Dad and their dumb rules!

But wait… now you are precisely the age that is more dangerous than any other age! The decisions you make now have the potential to make or break your life. Good choices will shape a good life for the future. Bad choices can devastate it. Understand that the majority of people in jail right now are your age. Why? Because so many young adults, keen to break free from the constraints of their parents, make poor choices, thinking they are exercising their freedom. Yes, you are free to make those choices, but as yet you lack any real experience of life. I was your age when I failed and was arrested. I thought I knew it all. I had a smart mouth, was bold and street-wise, but I was unwilling to learn and, of course, stupid!

If you're really smart, you will have respect for your parents, listen to their wisdom, be more observant of their lessons and understand life's pitfalls. If not, then you are a danger to yourself. Learn to listen to God. How can you do that? Read this short story that was told to me a long time ago by my Grandma:

A young man needed to travel to a city located 100 miles from his home for business. He knew he had a tire on his vehicle that was a little worn, so consequently he took it to a tire mechanic just prior to leaving on his trip. The mechanic examined the tire and told him that in his opinion, he could possibly drive on the tire for about 85 miles. The driver felt that the mechanic's tire prices were a little too expensive, so he left the shop without purchasing the tire and decided to make the trip, pray to God, and have faith. The young man proceeded to drive to the city, singing hymns, giving glory to the Lord, and thanking the Lord for the many blessings he received. Suddenly, in the middle of a prayer, he heard a loud pop, stopped the vehicle, and noticed *that* tire was flat and busted. He looked up to heaven and asked God meekly, "Why couldn't you tell me Lord, while I was praying, that I wouldn't make it?" The Lord answered rather quickly, "Son, I told you back at the tire shop."

The moral of this story is obvious: God is constantly speaking to us and he communicates to us in many ways through various people. What we need to do is *listen*!

Here are a few dangerous pitfalls that someone your age needs to be aware of:

For men: getting girls pregnant without fully understanding the serious ramifications of your decision. If you're not married, then you *shouldn't* be having sex. That's God's commandment, not mine. I've been guilty so many times of this sin and have fathered several children outside of marriage. Don't make this mistake! Not only will it devastate your life and the girl's life, but also the resulting child's life.

For women: allowing your God-given body to be used before marriage. If you're a girl attending a college or university, please be careful. A guy can always continue his education if he fathers a child, but if you get pregnant you will have to abandon your education to give birth. Save sex until you are in a committed marriage. If your boyfriend is not willing to wait for marriage to have sex, then he simply doesn't love you – period.

Making decisions without understanding the end result. Every decision you make in life has ramifications, for good or for bad. Never make a hasty decision, but always think through the consequences first. The object of life is to make good decisions that will deliver good outcomes. Of course, not every decision will result in what we hope or wish for, but we can at least minimize our bad decisions by learning from them and not making the same mistakes.

Surmising that you'll never need the advice, assistance and wisdom of your parents or loving relatives. This is a common pitfall, almost always made by a young adult who believes he's smarter than anyone else. If you have ever fallen foul of the law, run out of money, needed to find someplace else to live or experienced similar emergencies in your life, then this applies to you! Never, ever close yourself off to loved ones. We all have needs that can be best met by those closest to us.

Last but not least, *ignoring God and his commandments.* The moment we forsake God in our lives we have lost. Every good thing in life comes from him. God is everything and without him we can achieve nothing of lasting worth. No amount of earthly wisdom, education or reasoning can trump his divine wisdom. God *is* wisdom. That is his character. Learn to walk with him every day, surrender your life into his hands, and you will know success and blessing.

It's never too late to change your ways and do the right thing.

Chapter 18

Reflections – a Message to Adults

A message to police officers (and other law enforcers)

I would like to make a few observations based on my experiences as a police officer. In many ways a police officer is just as powerful as a judge or district attorney, because the officer is the person who determines the charges set against you. A district attorney can lower or upgrade the charges; a judge can only sentence you based on the charges; but the officer sets the pace of justice. How can a young police officer (in his or her twenties, as I was), naive and without much life experience, be given so much power? How can they be expected to be fair, when only a few years ago they were in high school? How can so much responsibility for honesty be placed in the hands of a young adult?

I've been asked many times at what age I believe an officer should be given this power. *In my opinion*, which is subjective, I feel maybe at the age of thirty. At least he or she would have graduated from high school and college a few years earlier and have some real life experience. If this had been me, perhaps I would have been able to say "No" to the partner I had who led me down the road of corruption. How could a young, inexperienced officer be prepared to make such choices? Can a young adult contest, outsmart, outmaneuver a forty-year-old, veteran partner? I think not!

I don't want this misunderstood: *I take full responsibility for all my decisions and actions.* I blame no one but myself and the evil that is so pervasive in the world. My point is simply that youth does not have the benefit of the knowledge and wisdom that comes from experience to resist evil and the temptation towards corruption. Furthermore, our decisions in life, at any age, young or old, affect people who do not deserve to be violated or wronged. Let past failures turn your future to the correct path.

I want to share a story with any police officers reading this. The reason for telling the story will become clear shortly. Near the beginning of this book, when speaking about the corruption present in the New Orleans Police Department, I mentioned the force's lowest moment, when an officer in the ranks was exposed as a "serial killer". It happened during 1995, while I was on the run. A twenty-four-year-old female officer, Antoinette Franks, was arrested for several murders. She has been called the first police officer to kill another police officer. She came to be referred to as a serial killer because she was found guilty of killing two restaurant operators as well as the police officer. Later the police also found a body underneath her home, believed to be her missing father.

Antoinette is housed at the Louisiana Correctional Institute for Women, located in St. Gabriel, Louisiana, and has been on death row for thirteen years, awaiting a lethal injection. She has repeatedly refused to be interviewed by psychologists, psychiatrists and especially authors or journalists. But some time ago she allowed me to visit her. She told me that she wanted to speak with me because she felt I would be the only person to tell her story, being a former police officer. First, we wrote countless letters to each other, covering a variety of subjects, then we arranged to meet – my first visit to a prisoner on death row.

It was a dark, rainy morning the day I went to visit her. I entered the prison main grounds, a mass complex of buildings and security points, and was searched before being escorted to her building in the rear of the prison, secured by many guards and chain fences. The security was amazing, though not surprising for a death row inmate. I was escorted to her cell, closely watched by a guard and monitored on video camera. I sat across from Antoinette. Her living area was simple. Her ten-by-six cell contained a small bed, a chair next to a table, and a toilet. It was painted a dull, nondescript color, sterile and clean. The shouts of other prisoners in the main courtyard could be heard in the distance.

Antoinette was tall and pretty. Her skin was golden brown and she didn't look like someone who'd spent thirteen years on death row. After saying hello we got down to talking about our lives. We spoke about her daily life in prison. She was especially interested in my writing and my life as one of Louisiana's longest-running fugitives. Although I wasn't there to talk about myself, at her request I grudgingly shared a brief synopsis of my past life. Then the conversation became more serious as we spoke of her past crimes and my past crimes.

The reason I wanted to meet her was primarily to discover if what she said in her letters was true: that she had repented of her sins and was sorry. I wanted to look into her eyes and see if that sorrow was genuine. I also wanted to know how much corruption she had experienced in the same police force I had been a part of, as in recent times I have been working with behaviorists and criminologists on the subject of police corruption. It was no surprise to discover that she had seen as much as I had, if not more.

In her personal life, she professed her faith and belief in God and Jesus Christ. She also maintained, for the record, that she is innocent. As I pondered her confession of Christ and ended our conversation after speaking for two hours, I exited the prison on this dreary day with a heavy heart, feeling physically ill. As I walked back to my car, I felt an overwhelming sense of shame and sadness.

Police officers and all law enforcers: you are stewards of one of the most important institutions in our cities. You have taken an oath to protect and to serve. You were not obligated to take that honorable and noble vocation, but you chose it. You are therefore bound, not only to serve the people, but to respect all citizens. In the past, I was no different to Antoinette. I violated my oath, dishonored my badge and lied to the people of New Orleans. I felt ashamed leaving that prison because, though I didn't commit any murders, it makes little difference – a sin is a sin. Seeing her reminded me of how sick and dirty I had been. Her predicament magnified my past shortcomings. I didn't judge her, I judged myself. How could I have committed such crimes? Why did I start down that sinful road? Could I not see where it would lead?

In the end, it took an encounter with God for me to see reason, and you need the Lord as well. As a police officer, your vocation demands you live to a higher standard than others; in other words, that you live a godly life. Your encounters with people should be godly, without prejudice, fair and, above all, sin free. You shouldn't rape, lie, steal, give out unwarranted punishments, fabricate or embellish, or do anything you wouldn't do to yourself or your own family.

During my tenure as an officer I took bribes, stole, unfairly administered justice and, of course, broke every one of God's commandments. Please, I beg you, don't walk down that road. Go to church, seek godly guidance, read your Bible and walk with God. I, as well as many officers, know how easy it is to abuse your power. Police officers can get away with many crimes and no amount of background checks, examinations, or periodic reviews can expose a bad law enforcer. *Take Antoinette's downfall (and mine) as a valuable lesson.*

To any person who has received injustice from a bad police officer, it's your duty to report them quickly. You have an obligation to prevent him or her violating your constitutional rights, your godly rights and the rights of others. I strongly advise parents to sit down with your children when they reach the age of awareness and teach them about the perils of police corruption and all forms of evil, as well as their rights to live as law-abiding Christians. Police officers, remember Antoinette!

A message to parents

Mom and Dad are the most important people in a child's life – the ultimate role models. They are the first people to touch, love and guide a child; the people most responsible for teaching that child. Parents are the builders of a child's character, the helmsmen of a child's journey through life and the planters of a child's soul.

Parents have an honorable but difficult task to perform. They have elected to bring into this world a fragile fruit, a fruit that needs to be handled with great care and delicacy in order to bring it to ripeness and maturity. It must be constantly monitored and gauged. Even today, I yearn and wonder how my life would have turned out had I someone nearby to call Daddy. What a wonder that would have been. My father existed before I was born, but strangely *was me* in so many ways before I was born. A father should be like a branch that bears and nourishes that fruit until it is ready to be harvested. A father, especially a Christian one, should be a protector, standing strong against any storms, dangers, or perils.

Fathers are charged, commanded by God, to love their children and not forsake them. There can be no reason, ever, to abandon your offspring. They will be forever lost without your guidance. I never knew my father and by implication he never knew me. I never felt his strong leadership or heard his words of encouragement. Why did he leave? What were his reasons? As a youth I felt I had somehow caused his absence from my life. This is a common phenomenon. When Mom and Dad separate, children often think it must be their fault. Children cannot innately grasp any reason for their father not being a part of their life.

No father's problems trump God's commandment to not forsake your children. Your purpose and responsibility is to *be there* for them. Otherwise, how will they know how to navigate life's rough and troubled roads? Do you think that another man will so easily love your children as you? Another may do it, with the help of God, but these are your offspring. You must ask God for his guidance concerning this great charge.

Your child's success or failure in large part rests on your participation in his or her daily affairs, but you must have God in your life to properly lead. Therefore, in my humble opinion, you are charged with making sure you *all* attend church or worship together, that you pray together, play together, eat as much as possible together. Show outward affection to your wife in the presence of your children, letting them hear you say "I love you", and make Christ an important part of your household.

I've personally visited the homes of the rich, as well as the homes of the poor, and if both are Christian households, you can tell no difference. God's love in any home is the same. My favorite Bible verse is by Paul, Philippians 4:11: "For I have learned, in whatsoever state I am, therewith to be content" (KJV).

Mothers are their children's heart and soul. A mother will love her children as much as the earth loves sunshine. If you meet a mother who has abandoned a child, you have met a mother with some serious problems, because mothers by nature are bound to their children's hearts and tied to their souls. Many children are able to show tender love more to their mothers than to their fathers. This is not to suggest that they don't love their fathers, but I believe it has a lot to do with the fact that they are well acquainted with Mom for nine months and somehow aware that she endured pain to bring them into the world.

I was aware that my mother existed, but I never really got to know her. All of my siblings referred to her by her first name, a telling sign that revealed there was no real connection. Yet, I still have a natural love for my mother and would have done anything I could to get to know her. Why do I still love her? Because every adult gains a part of his or her sense of identity from their roots, from their mother. To deny your mother is to deny yourself. I refuse to say, "I have no mother." Though we have lived apart our whole lives, somewhere during the nine months she carried me there was a connection.

Whatever went wrong in my mother's life that separated us, I don't despise or hate her. As an adult I accept that she played the hand she was dealt, for better or worse. Maybe she was an alcoholic, a drug addict, or just a person who failed to recognize that her children were more important than anything else? Maybe my father, or her father, abused her in such a way that she was crippled mentally and unable to take on that responsibility? Maybe she was simply an uncaring person, devoid of love? In the end it makes no difference. I still love her and pray that before she leaves this world, she might speak to me and my siblings and say something she has never said before: "I love you."

Christian and spiritual mothers are the cream of the crop. A godly mother would die before she harmed or abandoned her offspring. It's just not possible for her to live in this world knowing that her children are not by her side, doing well and being healthy. Even when the child becomes an adult, she's still concerned about them as if they never left the nest.

Husbands, you must respect this lady, especially in the presence of your children. You cannot, at any time, fail to show her respect. She is your wife and the mother and deliverer of your children. If you disrespect her, then you disrespect the family of which you are the godly head. If you have a disagreement, take it outside or delay it until tomorrow, but don't have a serious argument in front of your children. The moment they see it they will never forget it. It will set a pattern that they will be apt to follow in their adult lives.

A humble message to the clergy

To the Pastor, Rabbi, Evangelist, Bishop, Pope, Watchman, Shepherd, Overseer, Guide, Leader, Priest, and the man or woman who has chosen to take on a role that holds such challenges: you are the head of countless people. Please understand, I'm not preaching to you or attempting to usurp your authority. But you leaders are like the blade of a sword, the helm of a ship. You are guides to the blind and messengers to sinners. Your ministry has the potential to dictate the path of men's souls. If you're not right with God, then there is a danger that your position in the ministry is misleading innocent souls.

Recall the argument I had with the Reverend Thomas earlier in the book. Though he was right in nearly everything he said, his mistake was to argue with me without love. Even though he was correct in his statements, he violated an important rule of ministry; to preach and teach the gospel with love, not with anger. I was trapped in Jonah's great fish, but he elected to join me. As I revealed my ignorance, he confirmed his weakness in a lack of patience. As I showed off my ability to debate, he fell into the trap. 1 Timothy 3:6 says a church leader should not be "a novice, lest being lifted up with pride he fall into the condemnation of the devil".

Carnality and its derivatives cannot stand up against godly spirituality. They are contrary to one another. Therefore, my greatest message to you is to beware of lowering yourselves to the level of others, or settling for the lowest common denominator. Many would like to drag you down to their level, but you have been called to a higher standard, that you might exhibit true faith and show God's strength displayed through your human weakness. All of us are weak, we are flesh and blood like anyone else, but you have devoted yourself to Christ and vowed to resist the devil. As a leader you are clearly the target of evil and its devices, so beware.

You must also set an example to your family. Not preaching and then looking at women lustfully, appearing wholesome but double talking; not saying to the people what you yourself cannot manifest. Be mindful that Satan would like to trip you up. He is aware of your speeches, lectures and ministry, and is quite aware of the fact that taking you down would be the equivalent of taking down a hundred souls. So take heed of your flock and yourself.

A message to the scammers, swindlers and thieves (it's never too late)

The moment I became a fugitive in 1979 was the moment I lost my connection to humanity. From there I quickly descended into evil and became a hard, ruthless, unforgiving person willing to do anything and everything for a dollar. I called it survival, but in fact I was a predator who fed off the weak and innocent. I was willing to carry out any endeavor as long as the end result was that I won. But what did I really win? I used and abused many and all it did was destroy my own soul.

While a fugitive I observed no societal norms, had no compassion, love or ethical values. I was a wild force only seeking to devour. I didn't purposely set out to hurt, swindle or abuse any woman, but that was often the end result. I fathered a number of children on the run in the worse possible circumstances and sinned against them all, as well as God. God doesn't mince words. We attempt to differentiate and categorize our shortcomings, we justify our actions by telling ourselves that our sin is not as bad as another person's crimes, but all sin is sin to God. Most of the women I met in my life were decent and honorable, in some cases godly women, ready to settle down and have a family, but they had no idea that I couldn't settle down. An evil man is everything bad.

But it's never too late! It's never too late to change your ways and do the right thing. No matter how bleak your situation appears, no matter how hopeless, there is hope for you and your particular problems. God has a plan to solve your dilemmas and give you a new life – a life without having to constantly look over your shoulder, living as a criminal, dreading court dates, arrests and so on.

To those who are incarcerated, I want to say it's never too late! You may have to serve your sentence, but your life is not over. While serving your time develop a plan and begin to know God. Vow never to land back in jail again. God literally opened the prison door to Peter's cell and he can do the same for you. Just because you're in jail, it doesn't prevent God from hearing your voice. While a criminal and fugitive I could never see myself surrendering and my plight seemed hopeless. But God revealed himself in me and after twenty-two years on the run, not only did I surrender, but I gave up willingly and boldly, *having faith* that the living God, the maker of the heavens and all things, would set me free! And God did not lie, for I am free.

My message, therefore, to the people who are committing crimes, hurting souls, scamming, swindling and stealing, is repent and ask the Lord to reveal himself to you. My days *were* numbered and your days *are* numbered. The Lord is not blind, nor does he ignore the pleas of the innocent.

Are you a fugitive? Then surrender to the authorities and God. Are you a person wanted for a serious crime? Then seek God's counsel and do the right thing. Are you a robber? Then quit robbing! You alone started down this evil path and you alone have the power to stop it, before God stops you, possibly with a great penalty to pay.

*After my journey, freedom
itself is a success.*

Chapter 19

My Present Life, Faith and Missions

Many have asked me what my life is like now, since writing *Running Scared*. What about my faith, my goals and missions? What, if anything, am I doing to share the message of God's love?

As for goals, I have no lofty aspirations. I don't want to become involved in politics or be the CEO of a corporation. As Philippians 4:11 states, "For I have learned, in whatsoever state I am, therewith to be content" (KJV). Should God bless me with the ability to hold some influential vocation, I will rejoice, but I am far more concerned with spiritual matters and goals. I count my two greatest achievements in life as follows: that I found God, or rather he found me, after living as an atheist for more than two decades, and that I finally found true freedom. Compared to these, all other aspirations pale by comparison. But here are some of my personal goals:

First, to live free from crime and to avoid keeping company with anyone or anything that could be a threat to my freedom. My goal is to walk free, go where I desire, meet good people and enjoy the beauty of God's creation. With freedom I can enjoy the simple beauty of life: watching birds soaring in the sky and seeing leaves glisten and flicker in the morning dew. I love to look at lakes, rivers and oceans, powerfully moving with a rhythm only possible through God. I love the many seasons, always dependable, always on time, guided by the unerring hand of our Lord. I enjoy the beauty of the stars, so many stars, dancing in the sky. I enjoy meeting people who love God and seeing his plan for our salvation.

I am pleased that I can donate some of the profits from this book to various organizations caring for abused women and children. I enjoy performing free community service by mowing an elderly lady's lawn or painting her dilapidated home and seeing the resulting smile on her face. I love to speak, free of charge, at elementary schools, high schools, colleges and universities. For me to speak to young people without a fee is important. It validates my goal to be a genuine soldier of the Lord, helping young people to understand about God's love and advising them of the importance of avoiding crime and drugs.

I enjoy appearing on various television and radio programs and communicating in print, so that I can speak to people about my remarkable journey and let them know how much God has shown his love to me. I am also a pen pal to prisoners and encourage them to repent of their crimes, apologize to their victims who should not be forgotten, and ask God for his forgiveness. I tell them to perform some community service after their release from prison, to demonstrate their remorse for their past evil. For me, true repentance is not only asking for forgiveness, but doing something concrete about it. Community service is a good deed to perform after your repentance, because it benefits the lives of others. The giving of ourselves to others is so valuable!

I am grateful that God has given me the ability and knowledge to write two books, despite having no formal education in journalism. He has permitted me to work with two excellent Christian literary agents, Mr. Sanford and Ms Clark, both of whom I consider *agents of the Lord*. I love the fact that my work and life is surrounded by other Christian soldiers.

These are some of the things I appreciate and a sample of the goals in my life. The bottom line for me is, I just want to be a godly influence and a force for good.

Today, God has transformed me and given me a heart to see children blessed. I love nothing more than seeing a child reading their

Bible and the smile on their face when they understand something for the first time. It gladdens me when I see parents interacting with their children. One of the most precious treasures I have is my children and grandchildren. Through this book you have learned that many of my children were born outside of marriage, but though the circumstances of their births were less than ideal, I am grateful to God that they each have a life and an opportunity to worship him.

I want to take this opportunity to express my thoughts to them. My children, I'm so very sorry that I wasn't in your lives when you needed me. I'm sorry that I missed your first smiles, your first steps, your giggles, your tears, your pain, your first day attending school and your graduation. I've prayed daily that your lives may be a godly success, without the pain, loneliness and sorrow I've experienced most of my life. No good father desires to see his children suffer. I'm truly sorry that I've caused you such grief.

Likewise, to my brothers and sisters, aunts and uncles, cousins, nieces and nephews: I beg you to forgive me. I am sorry that I chose not to be a part of the family for so long, seeking first my own selfish needs and desires.

To my grandmother, Mrs. Tessie Jones, who died two years before I began my insane and unholy path without Jesus: I apologize to you posthumously and ask that you forgive me as our Lord forgives those who repent and turn to Him.

I also publicly and with great remorse apologize to all my victims – those who suffered as a result of my corruption when I was a member of the New Orleans Police Department and those who encountered me after I became a fugitive. Apart from my sincere apology, all I can say is that a new man has been formed as God has renewed my mind.

This brings me to the question of my faith. In the past I was a devout atheist, hateful of God and his Son. I spoke ill of the Lord constantly; I detested the whole concept of faith and salvation and those who spoke of it. To me "salvation" meant only to save one's skin, but the Lord has shown me how ignorant I was of his love.

What is my faith today? First and foremost I believe, without reservation, that Jesus Christ is the Son of God, one with God the Father, and the only path to eternal life. I believe that our Lord died for all men's sins and transgressions and I denounce Satan's claim that he should be worshiped and glorified.

Hebrews 11:1 says, "Now faith is the substance of things hoped for, the evidence of things not seen" (KJV). Many atheists detest this proclamation because to them, the subject of faith is like salt poured on a fresh wound. I too embraced that notion and exalted man as the only Supreme Being, able to direct his own path without God. How wrong I was! Without God we are not only lost, but entertaining and inviting catastrophe. Without him we will never find our way home. But through his grace he allowed me to find my way again and he can do the same for you. My faith now is concrete, the bedrock of my life. That is not to say that I'm perfect and never make mistakes – I still fall short of God's glory! – but, like the Apostle Paul, I strive daily with the Lord towards perfection, towards his high calling. My goal is that Christ would be found in me.

Lee, wherever you are, my friend, you were right. God is real. All the things you believed in are right, but at the time I knew you, you didn't have the power to trust in them. I want to find Lee so much, even today. I want to tell him that I would escort him to New York and stay with him every step of the way as my brother did for me. I want to tell him how God can deliver him, just as he delivered me. Lee, where are you? Have you grown stronger or weaker? Have you seen the power yet? Are you in need of a friend… a counselor… a confidant? I so want to show you God's way and see you set free from bondage. I pray every day that you are alright. Because of you I always try to look out for the homeless, the destitute, the sufferers, the beggars.

Father Clements, my good friend, my buddy, will I ever see you again? You became the closest thing to a father I ever knew. I miss our chess games, traveling together to various cities and your warm laughter. I only wish I would have done a little less talking and much more listening. Now I know about compassion for the poor, the need to express love to those in need, to be patient with the foolish and to share laughter with the innocent.

Grandma, I miss you terribly. My brothers and sisters miss you very much. We miss your guidance, your country charm, your sweet smile and your godly ways. We take comfort from the fact that we know where you are and that you are happy there. I wish I could see you again. There is a part of you inside me always. Goodnight, Grandma.

God has shown me so much that I'm obligated to help anyone and everyone I can. I'm not wealthy, but I am rich in spirit. After my journey, freedom itself is success. Recently, as I stopped my car at a stop sign, a homeless man was there begging for change. I gave him a ten-dollar bill and he stared at me in shock. I told him I loved him and not to give up living. He told me he had just arrived in town and was passing through. He told me I had no idea what he was going through and said it was hard living homeless. I told him, "I know exactly what you're going through, my friend." I gave him my phone number and told him if he was staying in town for any amount of time, he could give me a call. Sadly, he never did, but I will persist in reaching out to those who are lost.

After returning home, many people told me I should write about my journey. It took me several years, however, to realize that someone may actually benefit from reading my story. I understand now that if my story helps one person, then it is worth it. The final proof that God always led me is the day I decided to write my story. I sat at a typewriter pecking out words. I realized after one hour that this was too much for me. I looked in the phonebook, closed my eyes, and picked the name of a typist. My finger pointed to a lady named Carol. Her business was about half a mile from where I lived. I went to her office and asked how much a book like this would cost to type. She began quoting some figures I knew I couldn't afford. As I thanked her and prepared to leave she asked, "By the way, what's this book about?" After that I stayed for another hour as she asked about my journey and I told her my story. After listening with obvious amazement she said, "I'll do it. Don't worry about the money now. Just write the book." Carol and her staff worked tirelessly transcribing a portion of this project. God had led me to her. My life has always been directed by God; I just didn't realize it for most of the time. He will direct your life too if you believe.

I want to tell anyone reading my story to heed God's words. In life we will all experience trials and troubles, but don't try to attack these troubles with logic. Instead, put them into God's complaint box and ask him to deal with them. He will help you. I spend many of my days now in a certain local park, just giving thanks to the Lord. I sit back, enjoy nature, and constantly give thanks. If you ever see me in the park, say hello and we can talk about the goodness of life. I love this life now and I have finally learned to love myself.

All I have written in this book is true. I am not proud of these things, but it is the truth. I have often been told to omit this or that crime from the book. I could have done, but then it would not be a true account of my journey with God. I had to tell all because I am no longer ashamed; my God is with me. Many readers may still be curious about the "rock and can" story and the dramatic effect it had on me. I'm not! God acted in response to my challenge and humbled me. He provided me with unassailable proof of his existence. Now I don't need to go back into the forest and look under that can to know he is really there. That miracle brought me back to life. It delivered me from death. Why would I need to see that can? I simply believe.

I would like to say to everyone reading this book: don't be high-minded or selfish or arrogant like I was. That was my downfall. Don't hurt your brothers and sisters. If you don't believe in God, then *believe*! If you are already a believer, then walk with God, always. Remember the poor, the hobos, the homeless and the destitute. They are people with a right to dignity, the same as any of us. Listen to your conscience and be compassionate to all. My sincere wish is that you too will have a "rock and can" experience of God, if that's what he needs to do to get your attention. Keep believing and you will see the proof that he is there and he loves you.

Finally… do the right thing.

Your brother,
Robert

Epilogue

In October 2006 I was reunited with Father George Clements at a breakfast where he was the keynote speaker. Needless to say, it was an extremely emotional reunion. By chance, I heard the announcement of this speaking engagement while watching the early morning news briefs. I planned to attend this event and surprise him. Of course, he was shocked and amazed to see me after more than twenty years. In fact, he cancelled the original request by this organization to escort him to the airport following his speech, and asked me to drive him there instead. As we traveled to the airport, Father Clements and I discussed times past. We exchanged phone numbers, spent a few more moments talking before he entered the terminal security checkpoint, and planned to communicate regularly. As he proceeded to the terminal gate to leave I could see tears in his eyes. Simultaneously, I began to cry openly. As Father Clements disappeared into the breezeway, I felt I had lost a part of me again.

In addition, many of you may have wondered about the children I fathered while "on the road". Well, I'm happy to report that I was able to contact and reconnect with many of them. They were young adults or teens by then. They all met at my residence one day and you can imagine the tears, the laughter, and the questions. They now communicate often with each other, even though they reside in different states.

Information about Robert Leon Davis

In memory of his original victims and all the women mentioned in this book, some of the profits of *Running Scared* are donated by Mr. Davis to various women's abuse centers, children's organizations, churches and police foundations. Mr. Davis also voluntarily performs community service for many organizations. In addition, despite the many threats he receives from corrupt cops, he has joined forces with other law professionals and dedicates his life to revealing the secret and unfair practices of corrupt police officers everywhere. You may view his many police crime articles and details of his other books at www.authorsden.com/robertdavis.